MIND
THE
BOLLOCKS

First published in the United Kingdom in 2012 by
Portico Books
10 Southcombe Street
London
W14 0RA

An imprint of Anova Books Company Ltd

ISBN 9781907554469

A CIP catalogue record for this book is available from the British Library

10 9 8 7 6 5 4 3 2 1

Printed and bound by 1010 Printing International Ltd, China

Title font created by Junkohanhero

This book can be ordered direct from the publisher at
www.anovabooks.com

If, after reading this book, you discover your own bollocks, or wish to get in touch please
email mindthebollocks@johnnysharp.net

MIND THE BOLLOCKS

A RIOTOUS RANT THROUGH THE RIDICULOUSNESS OF ROCK 'N' ROLL

JOHNNY SHARP.

PORTICO

CONTENTS

INTRODUCTION

Hello reader. Come on in, sit down, pour yourself a drink. A piece of music is about to emerge from those speakers over there.* Open your ears and enjoy, for a world of sensual pleasure, spiritual invigoration and emotional solace lies within its fluid notes.

After it's finished, we'll have a chat about it. Then we'll read and write something about it. Then we'll watch a feature-length TV documentary about the making of it, draw up complex sub-cultural codes of living based on it, seek out the musicians to have sex with, get them to autograph our bottoms, then shoot them dead. After that, who knows? Maybe start a riot, a new religion or a complex socio-political conspiracy theory based around the aesthetically pleasing patterns of noise we've now become completely obsessed with.

That's the trouble with music. It's never as simple as it sounds. And it's not getting any simpler. Over the last half-century in particular, popular music has taken over Western and, to a lesser extent, global culture, to the point where anyone with more than a passing predilection for it is regularly confronted with questionable value judgements about everything to do with it, along with strange stories, fanciful notions and hare-brained theories.

It's no longer enough to make up your own mind purely and simply from the oscillations of air pressure that flow into your ears. Besides, you don't have your own mind – your every belief, perception and lifestyle choice is already hopelessly compromised by decades of sustained social brainwashing. You are little more than a dribbling puppet of the capitalist cultural hegemony.

Never mind, eh? That's never stopped music makers, fans and pundits alike continually applying spurious certainties to this most indefinable of art forms. Everyone thinks they know what's what with music, and they can't wait to tell you. They'll even say 'There's only two types of music: good music and bad music', before sliding a CD of Black Eyed Peas' lusty floor-filler 'My Humps' into their car stereo.

Meanwhile, we often hold the people who produce pop music (especially the kind that snootily calls itself 'rock') in such high esteem that we absorb their opinions and dissect their lyrical pronouncements with infinitely more patience and respect, and considerably less scepticism, than we would apply to the work of any politician or religious leader.

This book provides a wealth of reminders – in words spoken, sung, preached, ranted and written – that these people are as fallible and foolish as us wide-eyed simpletons who hang on their every word.

It also highlights some of the sillier things said about music by the industry that has grown up around the art – in particular, the music media. In our insatiable search for new musical discoveries to get ourselves unnecessarily worked up about, we are regularly bombarded with breathless recommendations from self-appointed arbiters of taste, while finding out to our dismay that the tune we just enjoyed on the radio is in fact a dismal example of 'landfill indie' (© all newspapers) and should be shot into orbit in a sealed capsule rather than inflicted on an undeserving public any further. This book shows you numerous reasons why these people (of whom I am one) are not to be trusted.

Ultimately, this book is a warning from musical history. It's a dossier of evidence to back up William Goldman's famous saying about the movie business, which applies just as surely to music: 'Nobody knows anything. We are all in the gutter, but some of us talk nonsense about the stars.'

Of course, the silliness found herein is essential to pop's enduring appeal. It's all part of the same stupid, spectacular snowball fight we can't get enough of. So by all means, continue to eulogise music, condemn it, argue about it, evangelise about it, and feel free to write your own book, blog or dissertation about why I am an arch-enemy of humanity's noblest art form. But remember, when all is said and done, to mind the bollocks.

Johnny

*OK, not literally. In future years I might be able to play music in a virtual room complete with comfy seats and stiff drinks via the medium of some book pages, but for now you're going to have to use your imagination.

Dedicated to the memory of Steven Wells,
the creator of some of the most inspired
bollocks (and a lot of even more inspired
good sense) ever to be written about
popular music.

The title of this chapter has often been applied to the output of newspapers. Another, less kind description is 'Tomorrow's fish and chip wrappers'. Or it used to be, during the antiquated era when most of the news was still printed on paper.

The same applies to music reviews, which means that dubious appraisals like those found in this chapter are largely forgotten. Or they would have been, had I not cruelly fished them out from the dustbin of history.

Music journalists and writers may not thank me for dredging these snippets up from the murky depths of Lake Forgotten, but there's no shame in it - even the best sometimes suffer from serious lapses in judgement. Including yours truly, undoubtedly the eminent-est critic of his day, who wrote for the super, soaraway *New Musical Express* under the pseudonym Johnny Cigarettes, and produced the searingly insightful report that opens this extensive hall of shame...

the first draft of history

1.

BAD REVIEWS THAT HINDSIGHT HAS CALLED INTO QUESTION

'If Oasis didn't exist, no one would want to invent them. For a start, they look and sound like they're long overdue product from a bankrupt Polymer Records Manc scally also-rans factory. Vaguely trippy guitar almost-tunes with vaguely late 60s rock tendencies, vaguely Ian-Brown-as-Tim-Burgess slob of a frontman, singing in a vaguely tuneless half-whine, vaguely shaking a tambourine, vaguely… er, yes, well, you get the picture.

But more annoying is the fact that they're too cool to dare to have a personality or be more surprising than the dullest retro indie fops, too well versed in old records to do anything new (e.g. a cover of "I Am The Walrus" and you know what it sounds like, kids), and evidently too few brains to realise that any of the above is true. Sad.'
Oasis, reviewed live by Johnny Cigarettes, *NME*, 1993

'*Thriller* is a very patchy affair indeed… if I was Jackson, I'd ditch everyone he's ever worked with and hunt around on the East Coast for some new talent. He has the skill, but it's wasted here.'
Michael Jackson, *Thriller*, reviewed by Paolo Hewitt,
***Melody Maker*, 1982**

'The (guest artists) put into action here reek of desperation… to cover the lack of inspiration in the music… "Beat It" is a terrible attempt at streetwise posin'… Jackson lays himself bare as a songwriter and the results are often acutely embarrassing… a barely developed artist being given too much artistic control.'
Michael Jackson, *Thriller*, reviewed by Gavin Martin, *NME*, 1982

Easily done, of course. And how could anyone have known what a phenomenon that album would become? Even those closest to Jackson could not have guessed how history would judge the whole project. Indeed, Thriller *producer Quincy Jones argued against the inclusion of 'Billie Jean' on the record as he regarded it as its weakest track. Jackson insisted on keeping it, in particular, the relatively long opening section, because whenever he heard it, it made him want to dance. Pffff! Imagine judging music on such simplistic dumbed down terms! Good job Jacko never tried his hand at music criticism…*

'I think (this) record is lousy… Johnny Rotten sings flat, the song is laughably naïve, and the overall feeling is of a third-rate Who imitation…'
The Sex Pistols, 'Anarchy In The UK' (single),
reviewed by Cliff White, *NME*, 1976

Cliff White soon became known as the man who slagged off the Pistols.
Hello from the man who slagged off Oasis.

'Were I an A&R type, I'd say something terminally crass like, "Sack the band, give the singer a publishing deal". As things stand, however, Radiohead are a pitiful, lily-livered excuse for a rock'n'roll group.'
Radiohead, reviewed live by Keith Cameron, *NME*, 1992

The headline for this review, 'Ugly with a capital U', accompanied by a quartet of distinctly unflattering shots of singer Thom Yorke gurning into the microphone, led to Yorke's refusal to speak to the NME for several months afterwards.

'Sloth posing as innovation? Not a million leg pulls away from an early Jethro Tull b-side.'
The Smiths, 'What Difference Does It Make?' (single),
reviewed by Steve Sutherland, *Melody Maker*, 1984

'God knows Rock & Roll could use some good old faggot energy, but… the sexuality that Reed proffers on *Transformer* is timid and flaccid… He should forget this artsy-fartsy kind of homo stuff and just go in there with a bad hangover and start blaring out his vision of lunar assf**k.'
Lou Reed, *Transformer*, reviewed in *Rolling Stone*, 1972

'Incredibly irritating… too trivial, too lightweight… one-song album.'
Lou Reed, *Transformer*, reviewed by Charles Shaar Murray,
***NME*, 1972**

'(Side one was) so utterly confused with itself it was difficult to follow… relies too heavily on taped sound effects of heartbeats, plane crashes and other insane utterances.'
Pink Floyd, *Dark Side Of The Moon*, reviewed by Roy Hollingworth, *Melody Maker*, 1973

'Neil Young devotees will probably spend the next few weeks trying desperately to convince themselves that *After The Gold Rush* is good music. But they'll be kidding themselves. None of the songs here rise above the uniformly dull surface… apparently no one bothered to tell Neil Young that he was singing a half-octave above his highest acceptable range… I can't listen to it at all.'
Neil Young, *After The Gold Rush*, reviewed by Langdon Winner, *Rolling Stone*, 1970

'The great Stones album of their mature period is yet to come… *Exile On Main Street* is the Rolling Stones at their most dense and impenetrable.'
Rolling Stones, *Exile On Main Street*, reviewed by Lenny Kaye, *Rolling Stone*, 1972

'The album has nothing new and very little that is even recent. The main sound is pre-*Rubber Soul*… And it doesn't matter if the words are sung as a put-on, they still are painful to hear… they are lacking in substance, rather like potato chips… The Beatles, though they might not have intended it, have in essence produced hip Muzak.'
The Beatles, *The Beatles (White Album)*, reviewed by Mike Jahn, *New York Times*, 1968

'(a) willingness to waste their considerable talent on unworthy material… If they're to help fill the void created by the demise of Cream, they will have to find a producer (and editor) and some material worthy of their collective attention.
Led Zeppelin, *Led Zeppelin*, reviewed by John Mendelsohn, *Rolling Stone*, 1969

'The kind of garage band who should be speedily returned to their garage, preferably with the engine running, which would undoubtedly be more of a loss to their friends and families than to either rock or roll.'

The Clash, reviewed live by Charles Shaar Murray, *NME*, 1976

> *The band responded by writing 'Garageland', one of the highlights of their debut album. And resolutely refusing to return to said garage.*

'Few memorable compositions… use of the wah-wah pedal is taken to irritating lengths.'

Jimi Hendrix, *Electric Ladyland*, reviewed in *Melody Maker*, 1968

'Mr. Presley has no discernable singing ability. His specialty is rhythm songs which he renders in an undistinguished whine; his phrasing, if it can be called that, consists of the stereotyped variations that go with a beginner's aria in a bathtub. For the ear he is an unutterable bore.'

Elvis Presley, profiled by Jack Gould, *New York Times*, 1956

'If you appreciate good singing, I don't suppose you'll manage to hear this disc all (the way) through.'

Elvis Presley, 'Heartbreak Hotel' (single), reviewed in *New Musical Express*, 1956

'Elvis Presley sounds a very mannered singer to me. His "Heartbreak Hotel" positively drips ersatz emotion…[his] diction is extremely poor.'

Elvis Presley, 'Heartbreak Hotel' (single) reviewed by Laurie Henshaw, *Melody Maker*, 1956

'Tuneless, heartless exercises in secondhand dancefloor dynamics and duff metal.'

Red Hot Chili Peppers, *The Uplift Mofo Party Plan*, reviewed by Charlie Dick, *Q*, 1988

'Their lumpy stew of speed metal, funk and street punk posturing doesn't improve with age.'

Red Hot Chilli Peppers, *Mother's Milk*, reviewed by Graeme Kay, Q, 1989

'*Leisure* is a quite engaging album… but it ain't the future. Blur are merely the present of rock'n'roll.'

Blur, *Leisure*, reviewed by Andrew Collins, *NME*, 1991

'Blur are praised for being more "ambitious" than their peers. Possibly because there's nothing much to them *but* ambition… Pampered, pilfered, *piffle*, Blur put the "C***" in "Pretty Vacant".'

Blur, reviewed live in New York by Simon Reynolds, *Melody Maker*, 1991

'Rivers Cuomo takes a juvenile tack on personal relationships… Weezer over-rely on catchy tunes to heal all of Cuomo's wounds. "Tired of Sex," a look at a brooding stud's empty sex life, is as aimless as the subject's nightly routine.'

Weezer, *Pinkerton*, reviewed by Rob O'Connor, *Rolling Stone*, 1996.

The album was also voted second worst album of the year by the magazine's readers. Six years later, Rolling Stone *readers had changed their tune somewhat – they voted it as the 16th greatest album of all time.*

'This man's muse is dead… I think it's time we left him to rest in peace. Paul Weller doesn't exist any more.'

Paul Weller, *Paul Weller*, reviewed by Steve Sutherland, *Melody Maker*, 1992

'A wasted opportunity if you're being generous. A shot in the foot if you want to be more melodramatic.'

Oasis, *(What's The Story) Morning Glory*, reviewed by David Cavanagh, Q, 1995

'It's clear the group's only asset is the ludicrously unphotogenic Boy George. God help 'em.'

Culture Club, 'Do You Really Want To Hurt Me?' (single), reviewed by Robbie Millar, *Sounds*, 1982

> *The record duly went to number one and Boy George briefly became more famous than Jesus.*

'Their "A" level amateurism is hardly endearing.'

Human League, reviewed live by Ian Pye, *Melody Maker*, 1980

> *Pye roundly dismissed the Human League's new direction with two new schoolgirl backing singers. Within a year they were at number one.*

'This album carries a sticker "Do Not Pay More Than £3.99 For This Album". It should carry a sticker which says "Do Not Pay Anything For This Album".'

Japan, *Gentlemen Take Polaroids*, reviewed by Patrick Humphries, *Melody Maker*, 1980

'If you're trying to create your own personality cult it generally helps to have a personality. Adam and the Ants don't… too much fuss about nothing.'

Adam and the Ants, *Kings Of The Wild Frontier*, reviewed by Adam Sweeting, *Melody Maker*, 1980

> *Within six months, naturally, they were superstars.*

'Greatness is never so boringly repetitive [referring to singer Ian McCulloch's claims and the advert calling it "The Greatest album ever made"]… It accelerates the unseamly [sic] slide of a once witty and occasionally inventive pop rock group into the swamp of pomp… dragged under by a swagbag of artrock cliché.'

Echo & The Bunnymen, *Ocean Rain*, reviewed by Biba Kopf, *NME*, 1984

> *Ian McCulloch memorably responded in a rival publication with the comment: 'It's like the manager of Rotherham United saying Liverpool are shit.'*

'*Purple Rain* is flawed throughout with a muso's megalomania – so keen to seem flash that any potential drama is turned to melodrama… soul's most sensual monarch jerkin' off to a soundtrack of faked orgasms.'
Prince, *Purple Rain*, reviewed by Steve Sutherland,
***Melody Maker*, 1984**

'Christ, so this is what John Leckie dumped the Roses for. Radiohead serve up yet another "anthemic" chunk of fey verse riffola and big Marshall-stack chorus action which will no doubt surf to the top of every college radio station in the US of A. But since we now have Oasis and they've been lumbered with Pearl Jam, we don't really care what they think any more, do we?'
Radiohead, 'Just' (fourth single from *The Bends*),
reviewed by Rupert Howe, *NME*, 1995

'Monotonous… flat, predictable… ('Superstition') lacks textural variety.'
Stevie Wonder, *Talking Book*, reviewed in *NME*, 1973

'They never pick the right tracks for 45 release… it seems destined to follow "Red Frame White Light" and "Messages" into chartless oblivion.'
OMD, 'Enola Gay' (single), reviewed by Adrian Thrills, *NME*, 1980

It went to number eight in the charts and was OMD's first hit.

'It's all over, isn't it? You can't base a career on one pair of lips.'
The Charlatans, 'Over Rising' (single), reviewed by Paul Lester,
***Melody Maker*, 1991**

As of 2012, The Charlatans are working on their 12th studio album.

'In musical terms they have a strong desire to emulate the '76-'79 bands… but the sound, while elusive and difficult to put a label on, is still fairly dull. The live evidence of the Happy Mondays is little more than uninspiring.'
Happy Mondays, reviewed live by Dave Sexton, *Record Mirror*,1987

'In an obvious attempt to wrestle hip-hop away from the West, East Coast critics have been gushing over Long Island's Nas as if he were rap's second coming. Don't believe the hype. Too much of the album is mired with tired attitudes and posturing.'
Nas, *Illmatic*, reviewed by Heidi Siegmund,
***Los Angeles Times*, 1994**

The album is now considered one of the greatest ever hip-hop albums.

'The majority of young bands are unsure of what they truly want their band to be, aside from famous. At least Muse also know they want to be Radiohead... perhaps Radiohead can start charitable donations of scrapped songs to creatively-starved bands like Muse... once that record [Radiohead's next album] takes flight, all the Muses of the world will become studio musicians and schoolteachers.'
Muse, *Showbiz*, reviewed by Brent DiCrescenzo,
***Pitchfork* website, 1999**

In 2009 MSN voted the album one of the 20 greatest of the past 20 years.

'The gel's stream of consciousness is running a little dry... Harry tarried as she opens her trap, talkin' rubbish you could call it (c)rap.'
Blondie, 'Rapture' (single), reviewed (in rhyme) by Ronnie Gurr,
***Smash Hits*, 1981**

'It's quite difficult to convey how bad this is. A slow, tortured strangling of some ancient Stones riff? Parodying yourself is about as low as you can get.'
The Rolling Stones, 'Start Me Up' (single), reviewed by
Pete Silverton, *Smash Hits*, 1981

'The title track... ends up sounding like Shakin' Stevens on a good day. "Everything She Wants", "Wham! Rap", "The Edge of Heaven" and "Last Christmas" are all better than anything on *Faith*. Maybe he should have stuck with Andrew Ridgeley after all.'
George Michael, *Faith*, reviewed by Chris Heath, *Q*, 1987

'Talk about fop music. This isn't just dull, it's an old kind of dull.'
Duran Duran, 'Planet Earth' (single), reviewed by
David Hepworth, *Smash Hits*, 1981

It proved to be their first hit.

'Could have done with a more distinctive lead vocal.'
Dexy's Midnight Runners, 'Dance Stance' (single),
reviewed by David Hepworth, *Smash Hits*, 1979

'The vocalist has a bad attack of hiccoughs and it doesn't match up to
the promise of "Dance Stance".... Vaguely disappointing.'
Dexy's Midnight Runners, 'Geno' (single), reviewed by
Kelly Pike, *Smash Hits*, 1980

Naturally, It went to number one. And the album that followed it?

'A series of interesting ideas misfire... potentially good songs are dragged
down by mannered vocals and would-be epic arrangements.' (5/10)
Dexy's Midnight Runners, *Searching For The Young Soul Rebels*,
reviewed by David Hepworth, *Smash Hits*, 1980

*Hepworth's future home, Q magazine, later ranked this among its list of the
100 Greatest British Albums.*

'I do wonder how long the Cure can continue to prop their songs against
the same chord progression, with its clambering bass and deadpan drums.'
The Cure, 'Primary' (single), reviewed by David Hepworth,
***Smash Hits*, 1981**

Oooh, about 30-odd years long, at a guess...

'Dismal, muddy thuggish trad-rock that adds further weight to the notion that Sub Pop is the hype of '89. These warhorse riffs are only fit for the knacker's yard.'

Nirvana, 'Blew' (single), reviewed by Simon Reynolds, *Melody Maker*, 1989

'This is quite good. Just.' (7 out of 10)

The Stone Roses, *The Stone Roses*, reviewed by Jack Barron, *NME*, 1989

'What could have been great instead merely bulges with promise.' (3 stars)

The Stone Roses, *The Stone Roses*, reviewed by Peter Kane, *Q*, 1989

'Now we don't get it wrong at *NME* that often, but this was a clanger. Rated 6/10 in 1989, but 17 years later in 2006 we rectified that early mistake by declaring it the greatest indie album of all time.'

2010, reviewing The Stone Roses' debut album in a feature about records that were underrated at the time

> *... and getting it wrong again – the original rating had in fact been 7/10.*

'If the Pistols really were the Monkees of their generation, as the Swindle movie suggests, then the Dead Kennedys are certainly the Archies, cynically concocting cartoon anarchy for the punk-starved States.'

Dead Kennedys, *Fresh Fruit For Rotting Vegetables*, reviewed by Steve Sutherland, *Melody Maker*, 1980

> *Punk-starved States? Didn't the Americans invent the bloody genre?*

'The music is a fusion of funk and rock and is about as enjoyable as a stomach ulcer. His feeble attempt at becoming a male Grace Jones falls embarrassingly short...the sooner Prince is dethroned, the better. (4/10)'

Prince, *Controversy*, reviewed by Beverly Hillier, *Smash Hits*, 1981

SOME MIGHT SAY
ME, ME, ME

'I think my album is the greatest album ever made…
it's even better than *Sgt Pepper* by The Beatles'.

Terence Trent D'Arby on *Neither Fish Nor Flesh*, 1989

… as opposed to Sgt Pepper *by Living In A Box, presumably…*

'Musically, we're more talented than any Bob Dylan.
Musically, we are more talented than Paul McCartney.
Mick Jagger, his lines are not clear. He don't know how he
should produce a sound. I'm the new modern rock'n'roll.
I'm the new Elvis. A friend of mine went to Africa. There
was no soap and no Coke. But there was Milli Vanilli.'

Milli Vanilli 'singer' Rob Pilatus, 1990

*The band were later stripped of their Grammy award after it was
revealed that they hadn't actually sung on their records.*

'Of course we're more important artistically than U2. And
that's not an attention-grabbing soundbite. It's an obvious
fact. And I'd rather die than deny it.'

Gene's Martin Rossiter, 1993

Well, Martin, we wish you no ill, so we'll just have to deny it for you.

'I didn't jack in Sainsbury's and sing with Shed Seven for job security. I did it so I could be in the best group in the world.'

Shed Seven's Rick Witter, 1994

'Once, it was windy outside and I didn't like it, so I phoned the front desk and asked them to stop the wind. I really was a f***ing c***.'

Elton John, 1995

'I met The Queen the other week at that cultural thing at Windsor Castle but she didn't know who I was. You'd have thought one of her equerries would have briefed her. She comes up to me and says "And what do you do?" "I just happen to have sold 40 million albums for your country, ma'am," I told her. My family was furious but I thought it was kind of fun.'

Mick Hucknall, 1998

'Firstly, I'm a genius. Musically, culturally, everything. Compared to the Razorlight album, Dylan is making the chips. I'm drinking champagne.'

Razorlight's Johnny Borrell, 2004

'It is like spreading my legs and taking a photograph of my vagina and putting it on the internet and asking people what they think.'

Lady Gaga on what it's like to put out a new record, 2010

According to a survey conducted by the University of Warwick[1], 100 per cent of the people[2] reading this chapter will not question what they are told in the introduction by award-winning author Johnny Sharp[3].

That might help to explain why stories, surveys and theories disseminated in the media and by word-of-mouth often get distorted to the point where they become largely false. In this chapter I'll look at some well-known pieces of received wisdom passed around about music, and assess, not unlike fat in a supermarket sausage, just how much substance they actually contain.

[1] I have a lower second-class honours degree from Warwick University.
[2] 100 per cent of the two mates I 'surveyed'. They both admitted they had skipped this bit.
[3] I am this book's author and I was awarded 'Most improved player' in my school U12s football team.

hit or Myth?

2.

CUTTING THE WHEAT OF TRUTH
FROM THE CHAFF OF MISINFORMATION

60 per cent of chart acts in 2010 attended public school, compared to 1 per cent in 1990.

Over the last couple of years, you will probably have heard this 'fact', or variations of it, mentioned on numerous occasions.

So can it really be true? Can there really have been a 6,000 per cent increase in privately educated chart pop over the last 20 years? Well, if you can take a quick break from whipping your servants, don your smoking jacket and retire to the drawing room for a moment, we'll discuss the claim in depth.

In December 2010, the *Daily Mail*, among other newspapers, reported: 'A survey in *The Word* magazine has calculated that at least 60 per cent of chart pop and rock acts are now former public school pupils, compared with just 1 per cent 20 years ago.'

They were referring to a piece in that month's edition of the entertaining rock monthly, in which the always highly readable *Independent On Sunday* rock critic Simon Price wrote, with no little dismay: 'The perception that poshoes are colonising the charts isn't an illusion. It's demonstrable fact. The official UK Top 40 of the week ending 20 October 1990 contained 21 British acts... Only half of one act in that week's charts – Pet Shop Boys' Chris Lowe – attended public school.'

By contrast, he points out: 'Of 17 British acts in the corresponding week's chart in 2010, two attended top private schools (Taio Cruz and Eliza Doolittle) and three went to fee-paying stage schools (Brit School alumni Adele and Katy B, and Italia Conti pupil Pixie Lott). A further two were grouped with mixed educational backgrounds: The Saturdays (two stage school, one Surbiton high) and The Wanted (at least one of whom attended Sylvia Young theatre school).'

'Only seven out of 17 acts', by Price's reckoning, were 'unassisted by privilege or patronage'. From that, the *Mail* concluded that this meant 'at least 60 per cent of chart pop and rock acts are now former public school pupils.' Hmmm.

In fact, the British acts in the October 2010 chart analysed by Price were actually made up of 30 individuals in total, nine of whom had public school or stage school educations, and 21 of whom didn't. So that's actually only 30 per cent, even if we accept Price's research.

However, his criteria for what constitutes private education was off-target too. He included among the fee-payers two graduates of the Brit School – Katy B and Adele. That school is not fee-paying, so we're down to seven privately-educated people out of 30 in the chart from October 2010. If we take those two out, then the true figure of privately educated individuals in his 2010 chart should have been...just 23 per cent.

Meanwhile, although he only found one privately educated pop star in the charts from 20 October 1990, it turns out he was looking at a particularly unrepresentative week in the hit parade.

If we compare the 40 top selling singles from the whole of 1990 and the whole of 2010, we find a different story. (By which I mean '*I* find a different story' – believe me, once you've spent an afternoon trying to track down which school Guru Josh went to, you will beg for the madcap thrills of cleaning out sewers for a living.)

2010's top selling hits were performed by 36 individuals, eight of whom had a paid-for education (four public school, four stage school). That's 22 per cent.

In 1990, 43 individuals were involved in the top 40 best selling singles. From those I identified at least seven who had a paid education (six public school, one stage school). So that's 17 per cent – and I could only pin down the educational backgrounds of about two-thirds of them. So all told, we can assume the actual percentage is just about the same.

And you might also like to consider those who made the charts but not the top-selling singles list in 1990. The privately-educated likes of Bruce Dickinson, Quentin 'Norman' Cook, Tim Booth, New Order's Stephen Morris, Ricky Ross, Justin Currie, Sinead O'Connor, Youth (one half of Blue Pearl and schoolmate of The Orb's Alex Paterson), Timmy Mallett, Lindy Layton, Sonia and Nellee Hooper. And guess who had the year's best-selling album? Why, it was another stage school survivor – Mr Phil Collins.

So in fact, in 1990 and 2010, there were roughly the same amount of privately educated people in the charts.

VERDICT: 10 per cent HIT, 90 per cent MYTH

Thousands of people audition in front of the judges in the opening rounds of *The X Factor* - and those comically awful ones really do think they're in with a chance.

It has become an annual highlight of the entertainment calendar to witness the scores of deluded fools turning up at auditions for the first round of TV talent shows such as *The X Factor*, announcing to Dermot, Kate, Jambert, Wincey or whoever is doing the shoulder-crying interviews that they really do have that elusive star quality.

We wince at the impossibly cruel circus of it all when they are sent before the judges to have their dreams ritually eviscerated for our viewing pleasure, like Christians being asked to do a breakdance routine in their pants for the amusement of the populace, before they get eaten by the lions.

Since the 2009 series we all thought it had got even more cruel when they added an arena audience full of gibbering, texting, twittering, 'lol'ing teenage twitgibbons. After all, it was surely humiliation enough to be exposed before 12 million viewers, given that many of these unwitting freak show exhibits are hardly the most socially adept, thick-skinned individuals in the first place. Before this new layer of public defenestration was introduced, their peers were already queuing up to jeer and spit on them in the street in the weeks following the show and generally make them feel like emigrating.

But in fact, it's even worse than how it appears on your screens. Much worse, and in any civilised society it would surely have been outlawed along with ducking suspected witches in the town pond.

Because the reason these people arrive in front of the judges seemingly convinced, against all evidence to the contrary, that they have some modicum of ability as a performer, is that they've already been told they're in with a chance.

What you don't see on the TV footage is the two or three rounds of pre-auditions that take place beforehand, wherein the production team spare Louis, Gary, Bobby Gillespie and all the chore of actually witnessing thousands upon thousands of similarly mediocre candidates first hand, by weeding out a small selection of auditionees to go before the TV judges. They will be a collection of the promising, the TV-friendly, those with interesting back stories (dying or dead family members, disabilities, unattractiveness, fondness for pies)… and, of course, the very, *very* worst.

So this latter group, instead of being let down gently and sent home from the pre-auditions at the first time of asking, will instead be sent through several rounds of pre-TV judgement before they are finally told they are 'through' to audition properly – in front of the judges, on telly, AND EVERYTHING!

They may well have shown up in the first place with a rather more realistic view of their own 'talent', but resolved to give it a go anyway. But as they progress through each round of pre-auditions, the validations thrown upon them by the show's production team allow them to wade deeper and deeper into an ocean of fantasy and self-delusion. Maybe they *are* really good! They're going to prove everyone wrong! They're about to enter a world where they are one of the beautiful people, now destined to prove wrong everyone who ever bullied them at school, told them they couldn't sing, and questioned their choice of spectacles.

Then they go into the televised auditions, their self-confidence falsely inflated to perilous levels, and we wonder why they look like they have just had a grand piano fall from atop a skyscraper onto their dreams. Still, I dare say I'll be watching the next series, won't you?

VERDICT: 20 per cent HIT, 80 per cent MYTH

Recessions produce great music.

'I hope the financial crisis gets a bit worse – at least we'll get a few good albums out of it… times of crisis usually bring out the best in music and fashion and politics and things like that.'

Noel Gallagher, 2011

When the word 'recession' began to win its tense semantic battle with the cuddlier, deep-breath-and-it'll-soon-be-all-over 'downturn' as the official phrase to describe the 2007–11 global economic nosedive, many a music fan made light of the situation with comments like Noel's.

Artistic creativity blooms in inverse proportion to economic adversity, claims the received wisdom. With fewer jobs to go to, more time to dispose of and a burning sense of indignation that can only be expressed through the medium of popular song, the disaffected youth spring into action, finding, as George Michael so memorably rapped, that they have 'soul on the dole'.

Yet this time around, hopes of a spike in cultural productivity from the general direction of the dole queue seem to have been unfounded. W'happen?

I thought I'd do a little research and try to work out if there is any correlation, on either side of the Atlantic, with periods of economic austerity and golden eras of good music. Hold on to your seasonal adjustments...

First off, I looked at numerous critical and popular polls listing popular music's finest moments since the 1950s.

And whichever poll you look at, it seems the period between 1965 and 1973 is a pretty strong contender for the title 'golden age'. *Q* magazine's 2006 poll of the 100 greatest albums has 26 of its 100 released between 1965 and 1973, while over 200 of *Rolling Stone*'s top 500 albums came out in the same period. Their top 500 singles poll saw peaks in the same era. Those were, broadly speaking, boom years in the US and UK economies.

Both nations' economies slumped between 1973 and 1975, around which time the charts became increasingly full of toothless middle-of-the-road pop and rock music, as anyone who has seen an episode of BBC4's series *Top Of The Pops 1976* can attest. Did Janis, Brian and Jimi attempt a head-first ram-raid on the doors of perception so that Paul Nicholas from *Just Good Friends* could cavort around in a bowler hat singing about 'Reggae Like It Used To Be'? The hell they did. But maybe people were actually looking for unthreatening escapism rather than edgy invention in trying times.

Of course, punk was coming over the hill to save us, but can we really attribute the new generation's vim and vigour to their electricity meter running out of 50p pieces? In some cases, perhaps, but most punk artists admit that the prevailing emotional climate that bred that musical movement was one of boredom, an emotion that is always curiously absent from the litany of gripes listed by people who are really in a grim spot. I'm sure starving Africans and persecuted minorities in Cambodia have not been overburdened with sources of entertainment, but somehow they've found more pressing concerns to worry about. Boredom is an invariably affluent malaise.

Furthermore, what probably made for a fertile artistic culture during those years was the fact that it was just about possible to live on the dole or a student grant in the mid-to-late 1970s without having to take on a crippling loan or face the muse-shredding terror of a jobstart interview. Maybe a little bit of poverty – or affluence – goes a long way. The next major recession suffered in the UK officially occurred between 1980 and 1982, largely as a result of the Thatcher government's inflation-busting monetarist policy. But did it really help invigorate the British music scene?

Some will tell you that the period that followed was a fine one for inventive pop. Remember all those cracking tunes? 'Ghost Town' by the Specials and... er... you know, stuff like that. Dexy's. Adam and the Ants. You know. All that stuff. The Human League, they were good...

There's no doubt that some truly splendid pop songs were produced during that time, many of them influenced to some extent by the austerity surrounding them. But in the broader context of pop history, the theory doesn't hold water. Between them, 1981, '82 and '83 can offer only 18 albums worthy of the *Rolling Stone* 500. Two of them are by The Police and one is a Chuck Berry compilation. Pfff!

Meanwhile, only one paltry single released in 1981 was deemed worthy of *Rolling Stone*'s top 500 singles. What was it? Why, Rick James' raging anti-Reagan polemic 'Superfreak' (sorry, I meant to say 'drooling, priapic funkgasm'), limping home at number 477.

Q readers were similarly unimpressed, with only five albums released between 1981 and 1986 making their '100 greatest' chart, and only one in the top 50 – The Smiths' *The Queen Is Dead* at No.11.

Maybe it's just that the kind of great music being made back then is the kind that people compiling modern-day polls manage to forget. But there's no denying that the public, the critics and the musicians appear to have accidentally agreed that the early 1980s were actually something of a dark age for timeless pop. I hope you're satisfied, Thatcher.

The next recession occurred between 1990 and 1992. That's

interesting, because 1991's output fares well in all classic album polls, thanks to grunge on one side of the Atlantic and 'Madchester' and shoegazing over here. The mid-'90s also fare well in UK polls – hardly surprising given the prominence of Britpop and trip-hop during that period.

But was either scene borne out of recession? Hmmm. The baggy era began during the Thatcherite boom years and while Noel Gallagher makes a fair point that when Oasis started in 1992 it was during dire economic conditions, the fertile artistic habitat that existed in that era might just as well have been the result of the aforementioned student grants, social security and leg-ups such as the Enterprise Allowance Scheme, through which you could actually get funding to form a band.

Even if you want to look further back to the beginnings of rock'n'roll, prosperity again seems to have been a far stronger driving force than adversity where cultural upheavals were concerned. The post-war recovery, teenagers' new earning power, increased social and cultural wanderlust and that enduring friend of vibrant pop music – boredom, were clearly all major factors.

So all things considered, perhaps we're wasting our time looking to the recession to save rock'n'roll. In fact, does anyone want to buy a guitar? Work's a bit thin on the ground at the minute and I could do with the extra cash…

VERDICT: 30 per cent HIT, 70 per cent MYTH

Alan McGee discovered Oasis.

When the BBC *Omnibus* documentary series profiled Creation Records boss Alan McGee, they entitled it *Alan McGee – The Man Who Discovered Oasis*.

That reputation is based on the story of McGee stumbling across the then-unknown Oasis at Glasgow indie venue King Tut's Wah Wah Hut on 31 May 1993 where the Mancunian quintet had supposedly threatened to smash up the venue if they weren't allowed to play. They duly went on and played four songs, after which a suitably impressed McGee immediately offered them a record contract.

A romantic tale, and one whose too-good-to-be-true quality has surely helped fuel a rumour that has since spread, which claims the show was actually set up by Sony, who owned Creation, and whose A&R department were already considering signing Oasis, or had actually already signed them.

I remember being told that as far back as 1994, and the rumour has never really gone away. But we'll deal with that specific conspiracy theory later. What we do know is that Oasis were far from an unknown crew of bedroom dreamers by the time McGee saw them on 31 May 1993. In fact, they had already achieved more than many unsigned bands could hope for – magazine reviews, a radio session, industry showcase gigs, big shot management and endorsement from Johnny Marr. In fact, over the course of the previous 18 months, pretty much anyone who was anyone on the Manchester music scene had become well aware of them. And although he may not have realised it, Alan McGee had seen them too.

After Noel Gallagher agreed in the summer of 1991 to join the band formed by his brother Liam and a few mates, he soon set about getting them noticed. Their first demo was reviewed in Manchester's *City Life* magazine in their Christmas 1991 edition (The verdict: 'Interesting, but I'm not too excited.'). Noel, meanwhile, was using the industry contacts he had built up through his day job as an Inspiral Carpets roadie.

Factory Records boss Tony Wilson was sounded out, as Noel later recalled on BBC Radio One: 'He went into a big speech about how the music business and the press was all overrun by cockneys, and how baggy had been killed by them all. We just said: "Right, Tone! Up the workers!" Two weeks later he rung us up and said the tape was too baggy!'

Factory's chief scout Phil Saxe later admitted to John Harris, author of definitive Britpop history *The Last Party*, that he was interested in signing them, but Factory were in financial trouble at the time.

Either way, Oasis began gigging in April 1992, made another demo, and rehearsed in the presence of industry figures such as Caroline Elleray, manager of Intastella, and Macca, manager of Northside, who were suitably impressed by the demo to recommend them to Mark Radcliffe and Marc Riley, who were then doing the BBC Radio 5 show *Hit The North*. A live session was broadcast in July 1992, on a night when New Order bassist Peter Hook was standing in for Mark Radcliffe.

'When Oasis came in, they were really stroppy,' Riley later recalled. 'Liam said to Hooky: "Why are you wearing those f**king awful leather trousers?" Hooky said: "You can forget about going down the Hacienda again." Liam just said: "Who wants to go down there? It's shit!"'

'I couldn't believe it,' says Riley. 'I thought then that if you bottled that attitude, you'd make a million.'

But of course he didn't bottle it. Many others had the opportunity, though, most of them the very next evening. Oasis played at Manchester Town Hall as part of In The City – the week-long event used as a showcase for Mancunian talent. Practically the whole of the London A&R fraternity saw them supporting Salford hopefuls Skywalker, but many were put off by the sight of Liam and Noel having a brotherly spat on stage. Couldn't they see that it would later be showbiz gold?

Influential Mancunian DJ Terry Christian (no, really, he was back then) was also invited to see them as a support act soon after and was given a tape, which he professed to like. Around this time Noel also passed on a tape to former Smiths guitarist Johnny Marr, who rang him up the following day. The two got into conversation about their shared love of vintage guitars, and Marr invited Noel to accompany him to a shop in Doncaster. 'I'd been to a couple of gigs,' Marr said in an interview in 2009, 'where they played to eight people and a dog.' He also tells the story of lending Noel a vintage Gibson Les Paul guitar which later got smashed over a fan's head during a particularly riotous show.

Marr recommended Oasis to his manager, Marcus Russell, who, in early 1993, began helping the band out, albeit unofficially at first. He helped Noel to secure a publishing deal, for which Sony and EMI were both in the running at the time of that Glasgow gig, having received four-track demos from Noel featuring early rehearsal versions of 'Rock'n'roll Star', 'Live Forever' and 'Columbia'.

By this time the band had already sent a demo to Alan McGee, so was it just coincidence that he accidentally stumbled across them that fateful-ish night in Glasgow? According to McGee, it seems he was in town to visit his sister Susan, and ventured out to see the band Sister Lovers, who included among their number a friend of McGee's called Debbie Turner, and who were supporting the band 18 Wheeler, signed to Creation offshoot August Records, at King Tut's Wah Wah Hut. He wasn't intending to get there so early as to have the inconvenience of enduring all the support bands, and turned up at 9pm expecting to see Sister Lovers. He wasn't aware that King Tut's had been given a late licence and there were still two support acts to see yet. Yet he also told the documentary he'd had 'four or five' pints before seeing Oasis, suggesting he had indeed got there pretty early, perhaps to catch the first band on.

Meanwhile, the story recounted for years before that claimed he was there because he had missed the last train back to London, and in 2011, he told a Scottish chat show that he was actually there hoping to get further acquainted with a model friend of his sister. Hardly surprising that the evening has entered into mythology when there are so many contradictory accounts of how it happened. Then again, the guy's not a historian – he was running a record company, not always entirely soberly, either, so why should he remember clearly?

Oasis had travelled to the show as friends of Sister Lovers (who shared their rehearsal space underneath Manchester's Boardwalk venue) having understood from the latter that they had been allowed an extra support slot. McGee had actually come across Oasis before, having attended a Sister Lovers rehearsal at the Boardwalk and noticed a Union Jack flag on an amp, which he was told belonged to Oasis. He later admitted that he wondered if they might be National Front supporters.

So maybe this wasn't actually the first he'd heard of them. Or maybe he'd forgotten all about that by the time he encountered them in Glasgow.

'I'd just arrived, and I'd heard about this band and how they were going to trash the gig,' McGee told *Omnibus*, 'and I thought "This sounds great, like the Sex Pistols or something".'

That's slightly at odds with Noel Gallagher's admission in a November 2006 interview: 'The story we were NOT booked to support 18 Wheeler is true… but the myth which says we threatened to smash up the club if they didn't let us on isn't. As anybody who's ever met a Glasgow doorman will tell you you're not smashing anything up in that town – particularly if you're five skinny kids from Manchester. You'd get your head kicked in.'

The notion that McGee signed them 'on the spot' is also somewhat simplistic. He did indeed offer to sign them, but Oasis manager Marcus Russell (who had also 'discovered' them, *after* Johnny Marr *and* Terry Christian among others) had other ideas, because offers on the table from other labels soon followed.

Meanwhile, there were complications in the deal because Marcus Russell wanted to sign Oasis to Epic in the US, whereas Creation had an international partnership with SBK in America, who had first refusal of any bands Creation chose to sign.

To get around this, Oasis were signed by Sony in America and merely licensed to Creation in the UK. It is surely this eventuality that led to the rumour, which has spread widely since, that Oasis were *already* signed to Sony before McGee saw them. There's no evidence to suggest that was the case, though.

So there's no doubt that a few other notable figures in music can claim to have 'discovered' Oasis before that fateful night in Glasgow, and by that point they weren't quite the friendless, unsolicited bunch of nobodies that the official version of history has portrayed. But credit where it's due: McGee did something which no one else in the entire UK music industry was prepared to do, despite having had the chance, and immediately offered Oasis a record deal. Fortune favours the brave. And if you look at the amateur video of that Glasgow gig which features in the Creation documentary *Upside Down*, your admiration will only grow – I mean, would you have guessed that this bunch of bored-looking troglodytes would even sell 50 demo tapes, let alone over 50 million records? For that inspired piece of vision alone, McGee surely deserves every accolade that has ever been awarded to him.

Obviously, Oasis had improved greatly by December of that year, as my review on page 12 confirms…

VERDICT: 20 per cent MYTH, 80 per cent HIT

The music press build you up to knock you down.

Ever since the Dead Sea Scrolls reported that King David's songs had 'gone commercial' and were no longer pleasing the Lord as much as they used to, musicians have bemoaned the media's tendency to praise them to the skies one minute, then slate them mercilessly the next.

On the face of it, that's no illusion. And it is due to one inescapable fact about all media: it's all ultimately about news. Then the news becomes any claim to the opposite of the previous news. And so on. Kind of like the following scenario…

STAGE ONE: BUILD THEM UP

The first coverage of a band will always lean towards the hyperbolic and excitable. That's because there's not a lot of point in writing the following:

'Hairy Plums, who are currently playing the pubs and clubs of Cirencester, are kind of OK if you like mid-tempo, just-short-of-memorable, I-wonder-if-they-might-own-a-couple-of-Arctic-Monkeys-records indie rock, but don't even dream of missing Silent Witness in order to catch them live. They surely have a glittering career of support slots to The Courteeners and downpage reviews in local listings magazines ahead of them.'

That's not news. You might as well tell us a hedgehog has just been run over on a nearby dual carriageway.

Likewise, the following review would be equally pointless.

'You've probably never heard of Hairy Plums. That is because they are, to be frank, cack on a crumpet. Their dribblingly generic indie guitar silage is really not worth seeing, even if you are at a loose end, wandering around Cirencester in a sleet storm bored enough to lick the inside of a deep freeze for kicks.'

Both the above reviews can be summarised as follows: 'This band you've never heard of are not really worth hearing about'.

So what kind of review would merit inclusion in a publication where space is at a premium? It has to impart some important news. So it invariably goes like this:

'You may never have heard of Hairy Plums, but by this time next week the whole world and her live-in lover will be queuing up to quaff their ripe rock'n'roll juices. The singer exudes the androgynous charisma of Jim Morrison being given a thorough prostate probing by Lady Gaga's diamond-encrusted electric sex truncheon, and the guitarist's mastery of the melodic arts make Brian Wilson's most sumptuous symphonies sound like Sham 69 being sick in a sock. The bass player also has nice hair.'

Hairy Plums (no, not *The* Hairy Plums, just Hairy Plums – get it right!) have been duly built up.

STAGE TWO: KNOCK THEM DOWN

Once it has been trumpeted over the hills and far away that Hairy Plums are the very reason why God gave us ears, the need becomes pressing to 'move the story on'.

The usual way to do that is to open up the field of discourse to the contingent who have been henceforth unwelcome at the Hairy Plums lovefest – the party-poopers who were unimpressed from day one and have spent the last few months wondering what all the fuss is about.

A negative review is now newsworthy because it is basically saying 'Previous reports were actually wrong'.

A common complaint arises that this squarely contradicts everything you have previously heard from that media outlet (and others), as if any media body, be it *NME*, Radio Jackie or bringmetheheadofbrianmay.com speaks with one voice rather than the babbling, bickering ruck of opinions that you would naturally expect to find in any group of music fans.

This sudden display of negativity often provokes the artist to believe that a conspiracy is afoot, and that this one bad write-up is part of a carefully orchestrated policy on the part of the media outlet concerned.

Obviously, the world revolves around them, so it's perfectly conceivable that the entire editorial staff of *Kerrang!* have sat in a meeting for a whole afternoon deciding on their official party line towards Hairy Plums, and everyone connected to the magazine is under strict orders to subscribe to that opinion.

It also appears this way because even when an artist has received 10,000 positive reviews and two lukewarm write-ups, they will focus squarely on the latter appraisals and moan in subsequent interviews about how they 'don't care' about all the 'haters' who are clearly part of a worldwide Bilderberg/Mossad-backed conspiracy to undermine their righteous quest to make quite good pop music.

And while one bad review might be considered inevitable, two represents a conspiracy, and three a full-grown backlash.

And so it comes to pass: Hairy Plums have been built up to be knocked down. It's a shit business.

VERDICT: 30 per cent MYTH, 70 per cent HIT

Brian Wilson, Bob Dylan, Prince, David Bowie - all geniuses.

There are a number of over-used words and phrases that infest 21st century popular culture like a plague of brands. One such word is 'genius', which has now been employed to the point where it is as meaningless as David Cameron starting a sentence with 'Let me be perfectly clear...'

It is particularly popular in music as an effusive label awarded to the most talented artists of their generation. And Pete Doherty. But it is a fairly reliable rule of thumb that by the time the popular consensus confers the 'genius' tag on a musician, they will no longer deserve it.

The problem is that people talk about 'genius' as a noun, as if 'a genius' doesn't just describe an individual, but partly defines them, like phrases such as 'a towering beanpole', 'a mouth-breather', or 'a homicidal maniac'. As if they were born that way and will die that way or, at least, once awarded the title, like a knighthood, cannot lose it unless they are exposed as a Russian spy or get convicted of indecent acts with a Shetland pony.

Let's consider some of the popular music figures with whom the word is most often associated: Brian Wilson, Bob Dylan, Prince, David Bowie.

In all cases, you could make a strong argument for saying that the description 'genius' did apply to them during the extraordinary creative peak period of their careers. But without exception, it sure doesn't now. None of them are producing work that even comes close to the incandescent brilliance of their peak period.

The reason they were given the tag in the first place was because they enjoyed a period of intense creativity, innovation and exceptional quality of output that was so dazzling that it seemed to be the result of some magical, indefinable natural gift they possessed. Therefore we naturally assume that its essence is within the musician rather than the music.

But it's perhaps most accurate to say these once-exceptional artists made music not in the status of genius, but in the *state* of genius.

And that state is, to one extent or another, a fleeting one. Genius is a fickle mistress who shows up, might hang around for a year or two if you work hard at the relationship and don't get distracted, but she's never been the marrying kind. Soon enough you'll get tired of having to do all the running and you'll come home one night to find she's shacked up with an aspiring singer-songwriter from Pontefract.

If we believe there is a difference between describing an individual, rather than their work, as 'genius', as a noun rather than an adjective, then we have to accept that no one is born a genius, and in popular music, barely anyone over 30 dies as one, either. Plenty of people have the accolade inappropriately thrust upon them, but in truth it can only be something that you achieve. And you're only as genius as your last genius record.

Why am I bothered? Well, partly because this myth is dangerous, and it allows those afforded the title to rest on their laurels, seemingly indefinitely.

As I type these words, Shane MacGowan is probably holding court in a bar, looking perennially about one pint of Martini away from lapsing into a coma, being bought an endless supply of drinks by wide-eyed admirers. 'I'd just like to say I think you're a genius, Shane,' they simper. 'Can I buy you a drink?' The fact that he has made precious few utterances worthy of the adjective 'genius' in a quarter of a century since The Pogues split matters little to those who are content to touch the rim of the legend's pint glass. I can't help wondering if a few more people had asked him why he pissed such a formidable talent up the wall, it might have helped him to get his act together again*.

Similarly, Pete Doherty made some very good records with The Libertines, and even as his musical output dwindles and his quality control slides steadily off a cliff in inverse proportion to the demands of his well-documented lifestyle, he has no shortage of friends and admirers to reassure him that his rambling, cack-handed, mealy-mouthed acoustic ditties are every bit as brilliant as the shabbily inspired and wildly original songs he wrote during The Libertines' peak, and if he fancies another quick chase of the dragon before breakfast, they can offer him a very reasonable price. They are not doing him, or music in general, any favours.

So I beg of you, pop pickers – genius is a very special thing. Careful how you use it.

*DISCLAIMER If all those well-wishers have helped Shane drink himself to death since this book went to print, then in fact he is, was and always will be a genius, I take it all back, and I am available for television interviews in which I will use that very word in several neatly enunciated, succinctly phrased soundbites in return for a modest fee.

VERDICT: 30 per cent HIT, 70 per cent MYTH

SOME MIGHT SAY
THE TRUTH IS OUT THERE

'I believe you can fly and I believe in astral travel. Because if I don't, if I thought I was just going to walk around this place for the next 50 years, I don't think I could exist.'

Richard Ashcroft, 1992

'Once I was sitting there looking at my clock for hours, thinking, "why is the clock unhappy?". And then it came to me – the clock was unhappy because in the back of its mind it always knew what time it was.'

Shaun Ryder, 1995

'I can see God in a daisy, it must be wonderful to be God.'

Bob Dylan, 1979

'More and more we are starting to wish and pray. The things we have tried to achieve in the past by flashing a v-sign, we try now through wishing. We are not doing this because it is simpler; wishing is more effective than waving flags. It works. It's like magic. Magic is simple; magic is real. Magic is logical. Try it some time.'

John Lennon and Yoko Ono in a letter to the *New York Times*, 1979

'Cauliflowers are a particularly pleasing example of the vegetable kingdom. You can think of them as lumps of dirt that we stuff into our bellies. Or you can think of them as living beings who have minds and would very much like to communicate with us.'

Steve Hillage, 1978

'I have a belief that if I wear my placenta in a necklace, there's a possibility of me gaining second sight – like being psychic. I would be wearing it whether or not I was in the public eye. I'm just honest about the things I believe in. For instance, I went yesterday to a past-life regressionist, and he told me that in my past life I was assassinated. I'm pretty sure that I was JFK in my past life.'

Ke$ha, 2010

'Lazarus, La's-arus, La's. He directed light, And the light comes from the water. It keeps you alive, la. And the pool is where we have to be. The Liver Pool. The Mississippi, the Mersey-sippi.'

Lee Mavers, 1995

'I'm not an expert or a doctor, but I think cancer is the result of undigested dreams and forcing yourself to do something that is not distinctively you.'

Sting, 2003

Merely playing music is not enough for the 21st-century troubadour. They also need to be able to sell themselves as a fully-formed lifestyle package for their listeners to buy into. That means they have to talk, sometimes at length, about what they actually do.

Invariably, they won't have been faced with that problem in their previous job, as a newspaper delivery operative, shelf-stacker or Government 'artist' (chief responsibility: drawing the dole). So when faced with a tape recorder and a pressing need to draw attention to themselves, they tend to fall back on tried and trusted soundbites we have heard from generations of musicians before them.

However, their pronouncements are not always to be taken at face value. This chapter is an effective guide to the unspoken subtext behind some of their more familiar utterances, as their artistic fortunes rise, peak, fall and, if they're lucky, rise again with a lucrative comeback tour a decade or two later...

WE JUSt DO WhAT we DO

3.

WHAT MUSICIANS SAY...
AND WHAT IT ACTUALLY MEANS

ThINGS ThAt NEW BANDS say

'You really have to see us live.'
Our demo is rubbish.

'You really have to hear our demo.'
Our gigs are rubbish.

'The sound/production really didn't do us justice.'
We're rubbish and we blame the producer/soundman.

'We don't sound like anyone else at all.'
We sound like a soup-bland mush of The Libertines, Arctic Monkeys and the Kings of sodding Leon, while managing to avoid inheriting any of the more arresting qualities of those acts, although we have added a hackneyed pomposity and some instantly forgettable hooks that are all our own.

'All music categories are meaningless.'
Which is why when we advertised for a drummer we put 'Indie/ alternative four-piece needs drummer. Influences Arctic Monkeys/ Libertines/Kings of sodding Leon'.

'Each of us has really different influences, and we all bring different influences to the table.'
The drummer likes playing *Tour of Duty 7: Race War* on his Xbox and fighting bouncers, the bass player is into Depeche Mode and hardcore Dutch piss-porn, and the singer sometimes pretends to be Michael Hutchence in the backstage mirror. All these influences are thrown into the mix, and then discarded, because the guitarist writes all the music and lyrics and totally controls everything the band does.

'We're like a street gang. The band couldn't operate if one of us left.'

However, if a record label were to point out that the drummer isn't very good we would replace him with a session drummer as quickly and unfussily as it takes the sound engineer to skin up.

'We're essentially a soul band.'

The singer likes to do his 'sex face' when hitting the high notes.

'We want to get our message to as many people as possible.'

And that message is: 'We want to be rich, successful, universally adored and up to our back wheels in soft, worshipful groupie-guts.'

AfTER ThE FIRST FLUSh OF SUCCESS

'We're the best band in the world.'

Or we were shortly after our last visit to the bathroom (sniff). In fact I could do with another. Can you pass, that, er, hanky I borrowed earlier?

'The lyrics mean whatever you want them to mean.'

The lyrics mean whatever you want them to mean as long as it's not: 'Harry Redknapp is an earthly emissary of Satan and must be destroyed, along with a shopping centre full of people just outside Aylesbury.' Because that's definitely not what they mean, so please don't make me part of your defence case in court, you screaming nuthouse.

'The lyrics mean different things to different people...'
But those people are all wrong because in fact they're just a bunch of random words with no narrative structure whatsoever that I strung together in the studio table tennis room 20 minutes before I was due to go in and lay down my vocal track, thinking 'these sound OK.'

'We're not being politicians, we're not trying to preach to people.'
We're not so passionate about our convictions that we want to risk alienating anyone who might disagree with us – that might stop them buying our records.

'We hate that sort of band... not mentioning any names...'
We hate that sort of band…but last time we mentioned any names we ended up supporting them at Northampton Roadmenders and they wee'd in our monitors.

...AND WHEN the NOVELTY WEARS OFF

'I don't understand why people think we're depressing. There's a lot of humour in our music.'
If you turn the volume up to 10, turn the bass right down and put your ear to the speaker right as the last track is fading out, you can hear the keyboard player farting.

'Continually comparing us to Arctic Monkeys/Libertines/ Kings of sodding Leon is just lazy journalism.'
Which is kind of apt, because sounding like Arctic Monkeys/Libertines/ Kings of sodding Leon is just lazy music-making.

'We'd rather people hate us than don't give a shit.'
… but we'll cry and gnash our teeth if you say anything bad, and put it down to a global conspiracy against us involving the media, the CIA and the fella from Snow Patrol.

'It's outrageous. They printed all these quotes I never said.'
It's outrageous. They printed all these quotes I said but then my mum read them.

BEFORE The RELEASE OF The DiFFiCULT 3RD ALBUM

(After a long delay in releasing it…)
'We're perfectionists, we didn't want to just put out something sub-standard.'
We were only too happy to foist any old tripe on the public but the record company demanded we included a couple of these things they idiotically refer to as 'tunes', or, more pathetic still, 'hits'.

'I truly believe this is the best thing we've ever done.'
I am so stir crazy from six months sensory deprivation cooped up in a studio with only narcotics, video games and skunk-addled paranoid schizophrenics for company that you could send me on a six month holiday to Jupiter and use electro-convulsive therapy to return my brain to a blank slate unfettered by outside influence, and I still wouldn't be able to tell you if it was any good or not. But if I say it often enough, and everyone around me says so too, maybe it'll come true.

'We played most of it live in the studio. I love that organic approach to making records. It was so liberating'.

We played most of it live in the studio. The record company love that cheap approach to making records. It will be so liberating when they finally drop us after the first single stiffs.

'We wanted to get back to basics with this record.'

We wanted to get back to selling records with this record.

'This record has a darker/harder sound than our last record.'

This record would like to be taken much more seriously than our last record.

'With this album, we could have just gone into the studio and made another (insert name of previous, successful album), but that didn't interest us.'

With this album, we could have just gone into the studio and made another (insert name of previous, successful album), but that scared the wits out of us, because we'd have to write more hits, and we haven't the faintest idea how we managed it last time around.

'There's always been a dance element to our music.'

The drummer always tries to do breakbeats in rehearsals, until we slap him in the face.

'We might not make another album after this one.'

Or we might remember that we can't do anything else.

'We'll follow up this record quite quickly and get back in the studio before the end of the year.'

But the record company think we should tour colleges in North Wyoming for the next two years supporting Bowling For Soup, then re-release our last single twice, then sack our A&R man, then sack us.

THINGS BANDS SAY WHEN ON the ROAD

'Make some fucking noise!'
We can't make you excited by doing what you paid to see us doing – playing music – so let's try this – it works in panto, so why not for us?

'We used to be into groupies but you soon realise it's a very shallow and unfulfilling way to behave.'
We used to be into groupies but you soon realise they have a very shallow and unfulfilling way of behaving, such as boasting about shagging rock stars and selling their stories to tabloids, which invariably leads to a whole heap of trouble with the missus, who still hasn't forgiven you for those funny little crawly things you passed on to her which you caught 'swimming in a river' on the last tour. So we now only do it in Europe and America, where the girls are far dirtier anyway.

BREAKING UP...

'The time wasn't right for the album.'
And nor was the place, or the artist, or the music.

'It wasn't the fact that it was a bad review... it was the fact it was so *personal*.'
It wasn't the fact that it was a bad review… it's the fact that it was a bad record, and we, personally, made it.

'Say what you like about me - I'm in a privileged position and it comes with the territory - but when they start upsetting my family/friends that's not on.'

Say what you like about me, but preferably with some reference to someone else, so I can use them as an excuse to have a pop back at you and thereby give the false appearance of being a) thick-skinned and able take criticism b) loyal to my family and friends and c) in possession of an ego that is not so dangerously over-inflated that it could explode at the slightest prod.

'They twisted my words to make me look bad.'

They twisted my words to make me look reasonably intelligent and able to string a coherent sentence together, which is no mean feat.

'We don't need a label, we're going to do it ourselves...'

Can anyone explain to me how this 'internet' thing works?

'There were mistakes on our last (flop) album, but I still stand by the songs themselves.'

There were mistakes on our last album, and I blame everyone but myself and my peerless songwriting abilities.

'We'll quit when it stops being fun...'

We'll quit when it stops being funded by a major record label.

FINALLy, the SPLiT

'We just wanted to explore other avenues outside of the creative confines of the band.'

We just wanted to explore other avenues outside of a 12,000 mile radius of those bastards who I now hate more intensely than a Third Reich parking attendant.

'It was down to creative differences.'
It was down to creative accounting, which resulted in the main songwriter earning three times as much as me even though I'm the real star and that ungrateful swine's own mother wouldn't recognise him if he leapt out of the deep freeze in Tesco's.

'I can't have those negative energies around me.'
I can't have the word 'no' said to me.

'The label never understood what we were trying to do...'
The label never really understood the concept of making mediocre records that sell like bat droppings.

FOR When it GeTs ReALLy DeSPeRATE

'I wasn't sure about appearing on the new Tweenies album, but my granddaughter said if I didn't do it, she'd never speak to me again. So that settled it.'
I wasn't sure about appearing on the new Tweenies album, but my granddaughter said 'Are you unemployed?' So I figured I needed to do anything I possibly could to remind the world that I'm not dead.

(On doing a collaboration with a younger, more happening young star)
'I've been really keen to work with (happening young star) since I first heard them.'
I've been really keen to work with them since I first heard the sales figures for our last album and my manager said it was this or an 'Eighties Extravaganza' tour of Center Parcs.

THE INEVITABLE
REFORMATION TOUR

'If we'd wanted to reform for the money we could have done that years ago.'

If we'd wanted to reform for the money we could have done that years ago, but I wouldn't have had the pleasure of seeing my hated former bandmates remortgaging their homes and begging me, as the most successful solo artist of the group, to get back with them. But now my last two albums have sold like second-hand pensioners' vests, my attitude has softened somewhat.

'We've got unfinished business as a band.'

We've got unfinished business. The band part of it is neither here nor there – it's a job. And quite honestly, we'd clean seagull poo off a North Sea oil rig wearing tutus singing 'Agadoo' if someone offered us half a million quid every time we did it.

'We never really split up in the first place.'

We never really split TWO MILLION QUID between us for playing a couple of stadium gigs. TWO MILLION. I mean, what would you do?

'The time was right.'

The time was right after a promoter had offered us TWO MILLION QUID for playing a couple of stadium gigs. I mean, what would you do?

'There's a lot of water under the bridge.'

There was a lot of money on the table.

'We will be writing new material.'
We will be writing new material so we can sign a lucrative new record contract and have an excuse to do more tours and make ourselves more money, and then release a new greatest hits featuring all the old songs which people actually liked, which will sell even more records for us and on we go until we all want to cave each other's heads in with cymbal stands, at which point two members of the band will leave and we can employ session musicians to milk the last sour, stinking drops out of this once proud cash cow of ours.

'We've grown up a lot in the last 20 years.'
We've grown tired of only having sex with our wives and four other long-term mistresses in the last 20 years.

'My songs are like my children.'
My songs are like children in a pre-Victorian slum – many of them died in squalor shortly after birth.

'We never set out to do anything more than a couple of shows.'
We never set out to do anything more than a couple of hours' work to pay for that new extension on the guest wing of the new house in Hampstead.

'I can't listen to that album any more.'
I can't listen to that album any more than once a night, which is how often I hear it, due to the fact it's the only one anyone wants us to play songs from.

I t's only a series of short logical leaps:

1. You enjoy someone's music.
2. You feel like you identify pretty closely with the sentiments they express in their songs.
3. You begin to notice that much of what they have to say seems to impart wisdom that you find agreeable.
4. You develop such faith in them that you conclude that everything they have to say adds up to nothing short of a design for life - a code by which you can find a better path for your own directionless existence.
5. They sing about jumping off a cliff.
6. You jump off a cliff.

That's why great songs are for the guidance of the wise, and the obedience of fools. Consider a few of these questionable instructions issued in well-known songs down the years... but don't *actually* carry them out, OK?

JuSt DONT BiTE it

4.

HIGHLY SUSPECT ADVICE
IN POPULAR SONG

'When I find myself in times of trouble, mother
Mary comes to me. Speaking words of wisdom
"Let it be... there will be an answer, let it be"'

The Beatles, 'Let It Be'

In summary, then: When facing any kind of problem, don't be tempted to actually do something about it. No, just stay right where you are, do precisely nothing and somehow, all those troubles will magically disappear.

Somehow I can't see that particular resolution getting past the UN Security Council next time they discuss what to do about genocide in East Timor or humanitarian catastrophe in the Horn of Africa, but that hasn't stopped many listeners imbuing this bilge with considerable significance.

On reflection, it is ever so slightly amazing that this pile of platitudinous hippy drivel ended up being played at the climax of 1985's Live Aid, when its sentiments pretty much summed up the polar opposite of what that movement was all about – actually facing up to a problem and mobilising people, *en masse* to do something about it. No wonder the man upstairs sabotaged Macca's microphone.

The song reminds me of an another oft-quoted proverb: 'If you sit by the river long enough, you will see the bodies of your enemy float by.' To which the obvious rational response is: 'Maybe, but you'll probably be 86 and wishing for death's merciful release from the chronic, agonising haemmorhoids you sustained from sitting on a soggy riverbank for most of your life and failing eyesight from obsessively scanning the river for floating corpses.'

But that's a whole other song. Probably by Sting.

'Bring your daughter, bring your daughter to the
slaughter. Let her go, let her go, let her go'

Iron Maiden, 'Bring Your Daughter To The Slaughter'

If you're going to make a radical suggestion like this, then you really should leave your target audience in no doubt as to exactly what you mean. But singer Bruce Dickinson leaves us in a quandary on this 1991 No.1 hit.

Are we advised to be the elder, instigating party in this familial journey to 'the slaughter'; or are we, in fact, 'letting her go' there, after she has badgered us for literally weeks on end for the latest *My Little Pony* accessory, a Justin Bieber calendar and to be allowed to attend 'the slaughter'?

Perhaps the plan is that she will attend the slaughter with us, and Dickinson is encouraging us to take a liberal attitude to parenting by taking her along so she can be inducted into the ways of the adult world, such as mass murder. After all, she's got to learn to enjoy genocide and unbridled carnage some day, right?

Or perhaps Dickinson is caught irretrievably in two minds here. Like a man with genocide-related Tourette's, he keeps spitting 'Bring your daughter, bring your daughter to the slaughter!' Then almost immediately, he realises the implications of what he's said, worries she will surely be caught up at the sticky end of the violence, and screams in panic, 'Let her go! Let her go! Let her go!'

With those kind of mixed messages splattered all over his scattershot rhetoric, once again those mums and dads who look to the UK's premier trad-metal act for no-nonsense parenting tips are left feeling badly let down. Or worse still, embroiled along with their previously well-behaved little girl in an embarrassing war crimes tribunal.

'Do one thing every day that scares you'

Baz Luhrmann, '(Everybody's Free To) Wear Sunscreen'

There are many slices of sound wisdom and, some might venture, bland, smug, and rather insufferable truism offered up to us by this 1999 hit from the Australian movie director. But on closer consideration, I'm really quite uneasy about this one.

You might spend the first few days scaring yourself by leaning out of fourth floor windows and going a bit dizzy looking at the pavement below, or flashing the face of Hilary Devey from *Dragons' Den* at yourself. But inevitably your fear threshold will rise, and your self-scaring exercises are going to have to escalate if they're going to have the same effect. After a month or so you're going to find walking out into moving traffic just a little bit safe and predictable, and will start riding your bike into the river or strapping yourself to the underside of trucks in service stations before they set off down the M4. That can't be a recipe for spiritual harmony in the long term.

'Load up on drugs, kill your friends'

Nirvana, 'Smells Like Teen Spirit'

Did I say that? Oh god, must have been the heroin talking…

'Mammas, don't let your babies grow up to be cowboys'

Ed Bruce (and later Waylon Jennings and Willie Nelson), from the song of the same name

The world's food industry can breath a huge sigh of relief at the news that relatively few 'mammas' took this advice literally, and many of them did indeed grow up to be cowboys, thus saving America and many other countries a beef crisis that could have had untold repercussions for the US food and nutrition industry and economy. It could have led to a serious influx of immigrant workers to take the place of all those babies whose mums forbade them to work with cattle. Wages could have rocketed, causing untold destabilisation to the economy, and we'd have the tedious prospect of smug vegetarians everywhere lecturing us on how much better off we all were for the continuing demise of global meat production.

'Love is all you need'

The Beatles, 'All You Need Is Love'

Hmmm. Maybe, but that's making a slightly startling assumption that 'you' have already sorted yourself out a regular supply of oxygen, food, water, medical care, shelter, care in infancy, clothing, employment… actually, maybe scrap that last one – breaking news just in…!

'Is it worth the aggravation to find yourself
a job when there's nothing worth working for?...
you might as well do the white line... 'cos when
it comes on top, you gotta make it happen'

Oasis, 'Cigarettes And Alcohol'

Some seriously contradictory wisdom from the Gallagher brothers here. Initially, we're looking at a slacker's charter, eschewing the popular notion that 'finding yourself a job' has any merits, even in terms of paying for essentials like cigarettes and alcohol. That's followed by a licence to imbibe cocaine at your leisure, slightly undermining their previous declaration that booze and tobacco are the only essentials in the protagonist's life. However, they then state in no uncertain terms: 'when it comes on top, you gotta make it happen!'

And after doing the white line often enough, you'll probably feel like you can do just that. Only without gainful employment to help you finance your habit you'll probably have sold all your possessions in pursuit of that next white line, and might well be offering your discreet services after dark near major transport hubs in industrial parts of town.

Along with your taste for booze and fags, crime might well be your only realistic option. Best of luck, then.

'Bengali, Bengali, Oh, shelve your Western plans
and understand that life is hard enough when you
belong here'

Morrissey, 'Bengali In Platforms'

Let's examine the effectiveness of the Manc miserablist's advice since this song was released in 1988.

Number of platform-wearing Bengalis currently resident in the UK: 14 (according to a 2004 report by the UK Immigrant Glam Rock Footwear Council).

Number who can justifiably consider themselves to 'belong here', given the proven economic and cultural benefits immigration has visited upon this country since the war: 14.

Number who have even briefly considered 'shelving' their 'Western' 'plans' (barely any of which involve much more ambition than making a better life for themselves and their families rather than, say, slaughtering every first born son): 0.

Conclusion: Jog on, Mozza you sad, xenophobic old quiff-teaser.

'It's the world's biggest dick - it don't matter, just don't bite it'

NWA, 'Just Don't Bite It'

On the face of it, this is good advice for anyone considering the act of fellatio upon a sexual partner with a larger organ. But then we find that this instruction is included amid deeply uncharitable passages in which the lady in question is told to 'Just suck my dick, bitch.'

We can skirt over the initial outrageous claim, given that the *Guinness Book Of Records* does not record the largest penis on the planet, and anecdotal evidence suggests strongly that no members of NWA would be among the contenders either way.

But considering how the protagonist is talking to the lady concerned, perhaps we should forgive someone sinking their teeth into the (pardon the pun) little prick and teaching him his own lesson in chivalry.

'If you can't be with the one you love, love the one you're with'

Stephen Stills – 'Love The One You're With'

On the face of it, Mr Stills is offering us an uncharacteristically conservative romantic philosophy on this 1970 classic. He appears to be telling us, as a recently widowed octogenarian aunt might, 'Be thankful for what you've got, make the most of it, and try and stoically repress those agonising feelings of unrequited longing for the dishy GI who stole your heart then did a runner back in 1943.' It's the kind of self-sacrificing ethos that has seen many a couple through decades of unhappy marriage while the true love that got away still lurks like a melancholy scar in the pit of their shrivelled soul.

But somehow that strangely old-fashioned world view seems at odds with Stills' free-thinking, free-loving hippy outlook. Could this strangely defeatist attitude be a misinterpretation? During the Crosby, Stills & Nash years, he fully embraced an attitude still very popular among touring musicians, awarding himself licence to 'love' whoever was willing and available at any particular moment, as a substitute for an absent regular partner. So this morsel of libertarian idealism would have been highly appealing to a man who was always reluctant to disappoint female fans looking to get a little closer to their idol.

Whichever view you take on his words, though, you can't say either approach sounds like a recipe for long-term happiness: make do with whoever comes your way even if they're not really the one you want, or shag who you want as long as your regular squeeze isn't around. Trust your uncle Johnny: It's going to end in tears one way or the other.

'Just remember to always think twice... don't think twice!'

Michael Jackson, 'Billie Jean'

Erm...

'Take me to the river, drop me in the water'

Al Green, 'Take Me To The River'

Ah... wait, no, hang on, from the middle of the Humber Bridge? No. Noooo! NOOOOOOOO!

The most enduring urban myths are both extraordinary and just about believable, and popular music has long been an arena where those two adjectives can happily cohabit. That may be why music folklore is packed with eyebrow-raising 'facts', jaw-dropping anecdotes and dubious yarns that invariably only enhance the reputations of the artists concerned. A Conservative councillor might find his career in trouble after rumours spread regarding his unorthodox sexual practices with popular confectionery, but the same can rarely be said of musicians.

So, in this chapter there is a choice selection of well-worn stories that have been widely spread among lists of 10/20/50 facts you 'didn't know' about music. And as it turns out, you *still* don't know them, because they're all untrue...

URBAN MyThS

5.

WHEN BOLLOCKS GOES VIRAL

Charles Manson auditioned for The Monkees.

This gem used to be reported regularly among lists of things you supposedly 'didn't know' about both Manson and The Monkees, until the age of the internet helped disseminate the truth, which was that Manson was in jail between 1960 and 1967, so he could not possibly have attended the auditions in September 1965. He would also have been 30, and therefore too old to apply for the job.

10cc were named after the average amount of male ejaculate.

During the hit-making prime of the Mancunian MOR quartet, it was widely reported – and still is – that their name was derived from the above source. In fact, original manager Jonathan King gave them the name after claiming he saw the words lit up in a dream. Besides, the average amount of male ejaculate is actually around 3cc.

Rod Stewart/Marc Almond/Elton John collapsed at a party and had several litres of male semen pumped from their stomach.

An enduring favourite in playgrounds on both sides of the Atlantic for years, the subject has changed (invariably an effeminate rock star who is thought to be homosexual, but sometimes also featuring a lusted-after female popstrel of the day), but some details endure: the collapse, the stomach pump and the semen.

Once again, the colourful nature of the story negates the need to scrutinise the details. Because that would reveal that a) semen is not harmful or toxic if consumed and b) they would have had to fellate half the population of Shrewsbury, even if they were producing 10cc-worthy amounts of love snot.

Deborah Harry was almost murdered by Ted Bundy.

The Blondie singer has often told a tale of being offered a lift by a stranger in New York in the early 1970s. When she got in she found a stripped out interior seemingly designed to prevent the occupant from getting out. She escaped by operating the door handle from the outside, and has since said she is convinced that Bundy, who confessed to murdering at least 30 women, was the mysterious stranger.

No doubt it was a real and terrifying incident, but further investigation suggests it couldn't have involved Bundy. He never set foot anywhere near New York throughout the 1970s, and his car didn't match the description she gave.

Keith Richards had his blood changed.

The Stones guitarist's unrivalled reputation for supernatural endurance was enhanced by his story that he twice had a blood transfusion to the clean, non-heroin addicted variety at a Swiss clinic in order to get off smack in the 1970s. Victor Bockris's biography of the great man claims he underwent the operation twice, once to obtain a US visa in 1975, but since then Richards himself has admitted that he made up these stories just to humour people when they kept asking him how he kicked the junk.

There is a sonic frequency known as 'the brown note' that has been used to induce vomiting, defecation and temporary unconsciousness in anyone who hears it.

New York sonic terrorists Swans are reputed to have performed at such volume at one London show in 1987 that they made some fans' ears bleed and induced vomiting in others. Mind you, if you'd tasted the beer at some of these venues...

In 2005, Discovery Channel TV series *Mythbusters* even tried out frequencies between 5 and 20Hz at volumes over 120 decibels, and although the presenters felt blurred vision due to vibration of their eyeballs from such low frequencies, their undercrackers remained resolutely clean and their lunch remained firmly *in situ*.

The truth is so *bloody* boring, isn't it?

Bono was heckled - amusingly - for saying 'Every time I clap my hands, a child dies'.

The story goes that everyone's favourite globetrotting politician and occasional rock frontman, Bono, stopped a U2 show and began clicking his fingers slowly and rhythmically.

'Every time I click my fingers,' he supposedly said, 'a child dies of starvation in Africa.'

Immediately, a heckle from the crowd responded, 'well stop clicking your fingers, then!'

Alas, in the real world, no one is quite that spontaneously witty. Especially in the front rows of a U2 arena show.

Finger-clicking was indeed performed by Bono, among others, during the 2005 Make Poverty History campaign, which featured a string of celebrities (Bono included) clicking their fingers in a slow rhythm, with the voiceover, 'A child dies completely unnecessarily from extreme poverty every three seconds.'

Jimmy Carr later commented in his live act, 'I saw those ads and I couldn't help thinking "Well, stop clicking your fingers".'

The story has since been retold starring everyone from Barack Obama to Fearne Cotton, and continues to help mean-spirited cretins everywhere feel a bit more smug about telling charity campaigners where they can stick their do-gooding.

Marilyn Manson played 'Paul' in *The Wonder Years*.

Amazingly, this rumour spread like wildfire when the God of F**k had his first flush of success. I suppose it was possible that his real name might have been Josh Saviano (sounds better than Brian Warner). But why did no one think to glance at his date of birth, 1969, which would put him at age 19 (playing a pre-pubescent) during the first series?

Marilyn Manson had a rib removed so he could fellate himself.

A tempting option for any male rock star for whom money was no option. Alas, he wasn't that desperate. In our Brian's autobiography *The Long Hard Road Out of Hell* he comments, 'If I really got my ribs removed, I would have been busy sucking my own dick on *The Wonder Years* instead of chasing Winnie Cooper.'

Blockbusters presenter Bob Holness played the iconic saxophone break on Gerry Rafferty's 'Baker Street'.

The beauty of this prize morsel of poppycock is that it sounds just plausible enough to believe, while also being unlikely enough to be worth spreading far and wide, and just too obscure for anyone to bother looking into. Or at least, they didn't around the time when this assertion was first made, in the 'Believe it or not!' section of *NME's* satirical 'Thrills' page in 1990, as a spoof of media 'Did you know… ' lists.

Stevie Nicks employed a roadie to blow cocaine up her bum.

The story has it that at one point, the erstwhile Fleetwood Mac warbler had done so much damage to her hooter that she could no longer use it for the intake of the devil's dandruff. So Stevie duly employed a roadie whose sole function on tour was to blow cocaine up Ms Nicks' Khyber pass with a straw, thus allowing her to maintain her high at all times.

Aside from the tell-tale absence of any eye witnesses to such activity, and amused denial of any and all Mac road crew operatives of any such chores (then again, if you were the roadie tasked with the job, would you admit it?) we also have to bear in mind that the disappearance of her septum wouldn't normally prevent her from taking the drug orally (rubbed on the gums for instance). So sorry, you can stick that one… anywhere you like, really.

Queen had a party where cocaine was carried around on trays on dwarves' heads.

All the surviving members of Queen deny this took place at an 'infamous' party in New Orleans in 1978 as a launch do for their album *Jazz*. No one else who was at the do has said they saw it either, according to Queen biographer Mark Blake. Now, if this was a notorious gangland massacre taking place, lack of witnesses would not mean it didn't happen. But surely the story of 'rock band on tour employ novel method of taking lots of drugs' wouldn't be shameful enough to deny it if it was true, right?

The Beatles smoked a spliff in the Buckingham Palace toilets before receiving their MBEs.

When The Beatles received their MBEs from the Queen in 1965, some were so outraged that they returned their own honours in protest. But they probably would have crapped in an envelope and sent it direct to the Palace if they'd caught wind of what John Lennon later claimed to have been up to that day.

In a 1970 interview he said that when they met the monarch, '[we] were giggling like crazy because we had just smoked a joint in the loos of Buckingham Palace.'

A cracking story, but some years later, George Harrison offered a rather less sensational version of events.

'We were so nervous that we went to the toilet,' he explained. 'And in there we smoked a cigarette. Years later, I'm sure John was thinking back and remembering, "Oh yes, we went in the toilet and smoked," and it turned into a reefer. Because what could be the worst thing you could do before you meet the Queen? Smoke a reefer! But we never did.'

Trust George to be the boring one and ruin all our illusions.

Phil Collins wrote 'In The Air Tonight' about witnessing a drowning, and later sang it to the man involved in the front row at his concert.

'Well if you told me you were drowning, I would not lend a hand.' So goes a prominent line in Phil Collins' breakthrough solo hit. In the years following its release, a story spread that claimed the song was written about a true incident. Collins, they said, had witnessed a man watching another man drown, without trying to help him. He then found out the identity of this individual and sent him free front row tickets to his next show, where he sang the song directly to the guilty party as he was bathed in spotlight.

Alas, it's all rubbish. There was no drowning, Collins just wanted to have a pop at his wife for leaving him for the bloke who was decorating their house. Anyway, I knew this story was too good to be true – he's not that nice a bloke. And didn't he do something really horrible to his next wife… ?

Phil Collins divorced his second wife by fax.

Not quite. They were already getting divorced when he sent her a snotty fax about dividing up their possessions and access to their kids.

Collins told the *Radio Times* in 2002, 'I was touring in Germany, trying to workout access to Lily. Jill was angry and kept putting the phone down so I wrote her another fax, which was printed on the front page of *The Sun* the next day.'

Oh well, I'm still not having it. Didn't he threaten to... oh, yeah...

Phil Collins once threatened to leave the country if Labour got elected...

Let's let Phil clear this one up. Speaking to that bastion of truth and decency, the *Daily Mail*, he said he hadn't voted since 1969 anyway, and as for leaving the country...

'I moved to Switzerland (in 1994) because I'd fallen in love with a woman who lived on Lake Geneva. As I said at the time, I'd have moved to Grimsby if she happened to live there. Inevitably, everyone in Grimsby turned around and said, "Why's he having a pop at Grimsby?" If you're Phil Collins it seems you just can't win.'

Oh stop moaning Phil, anyone would think I'd written half this chapter about you.

The guitarist from INXS severed his penis while fishing.

Australia's favourite (only?) funk-rockers were no strangers to furry folklore thanks to the well-documented lifestyle tendencies of their late singer. But even Michael Hutchence at his hoariest would struggle to outdo the band's guitarist, Kirk Pengilly, who was out fishing near his home early one morning when the most horrifying disaster befell him.

Wearing only a skimpy pair of shorts, he set about cutting up a fish he had caught when the knife slipped, and sliced straight through his pride and joy. Whether he was entirely sober is one for future generations to ponder, but suffice it to say that had it not been for a generous consignment of ice cubes and a very quick trip to hospital for an emergency re-attachment operation, his guitar would be more than just a symbolic phallic substitute.

'There comes a point in every band or artist's life when they have had quite enough of answering the same old questions about how they met, how they got their name, whether they were 'surprised' at ending up at number 13 in the singles charts, and what *really* happened in the swimming pool at Benicassim that time with the Alpaca, the mound of Miaow Miaow and the Portuguese ladyboy.

Sooner or later, artists discover the ancient truth that the real story is far too mundane for the media to take any interest in, so in order to enhance their chances of getting the press coverage they want, they themselves resort to making stuff up.

Here's a few tall tales of self promotion that have been cut down to size over the years...

fiction factory

6.

LIES, EXAGGERATION AND SELF-PROMOTION

FIB The White Stripes' Jack and Meg White are brother and sister.

FACT Jack and Meg were actually husband and wife, but understandably wanted to avoid all those tedious relationship questions during their initial media encounters, especially as their divorce had been finalised in March 2000, shortly before they became well known.

In 2005 Jack told *Rolling Stone*: 'When they're brother and sister, you go, "Oh, that's interesting." You care more about the music, not the relationship – whether they're trying to save their relationship by being in a band.'

FIB The Stone Roses' Ian Brown once insisted on being called 'King Monkey'.

FACT During the Roses' long early '90s hiatus, speculation mounted as to how the baggy heroes were getting on with making the follow-up to their self-titled 1989 debut. However, their camp was shrouded in secrecy, and in desperation, journalists turned to some not entirely reliable sources for information. One who was refreshingly keen to talk was Matthew Priest, drummer with Midlands melodians Dodgy. He told the *Guardian* that he had been a witness to rehearsals and claimed that not only had the Roses performed a reggae version of The Eagles' 'Hotel California', but that Ian Brown was now insisting on being addressed as 'King Monkey,' and refused to answer to any other name.

All shameless fabrication, unfortunately, but it did at least amuse Brown himself when he read the story, and he later referred to it when calling his debut solo album *Unfinished Monkey Business*.

FIB The Hives' songs were written by a mysterious svengali named Randy Fitzsimmons.

FACT Ever since their formation in Fagersta, Sweden, in 1993, garage rock quintet The Hives have insisted that their management, musical direction, visual image, band name and even songwriting were all orchestrated by a 'sixth member' of the band, a reclusive individual named Randy Fitzsimmons. He originally formed the band, they continue to insist, by sending each member a letter asking them to meet at a given time and place.

However, *NME* revealed in 2004 that after checking with the Performer's Rights Society, they had proof that Fitzsimmons was a pseudonym for guitarist Nicholaus 'Arson' Almqvist. A simple misunderstanding, explained the band. Almqvist picks up Fitzsimmons' cheques to take advantage of a tax loophole.

In a line of work where 99.9 per cent of real manufactured pop stars are at pains to stress their own involvement in the creative process (just how much did all those reality show singers do to earn those co-writers' credits, one wonders?), it's quite refreshing to find a band insisting the opposite.

And can we really be sure that Randy is a figment of their imagination? After all, on the back sleeve of their 2004 album *Tyrannosaurus Hives* there are six pairs of legs, while in the video for 'Main Offender' his hand is shown signing a contract.

Rock's longest-running, and best ever lie? It gets my vote.

FIB   The Clash – 'Daddy Was A Bank Robber'.

FACT   At the time when this record was released, we didn't have the internet to make it a simple task for nosy journos or inquisitive fans to delve into a musician's background. But even back then it was soon established that contrary to the titular claim, Joe Strummer, who wrote the line in question, had a daddy who was a high-ranking diplomat. His explanation, employed by many hundreds of musicians since then when using a more dangerous back story to glorify their own in song, is that he was singing in character. Whether he would have admitted this if he hadn't been called out on it is one of pop music's eternal imponderables.

FIB   The late James Brown told a female employee that the government had implanted him with bull's testicles to preserve his sexual prowess forever.

FACT   This startling allegation was made in a 2002 lawsuit taken against the Godfather of Soul. Unfortunately, the claim, made by 36-year-old

Lisa Agbalaya, formed part of a case for wrongful dismissal that was ultimately unsuccessful. Scientists, meanwhile, have still to perform the first bull-to-human testicular transplant operation – unless the government – and the erstwhile Minister Of New New Super Heavy Funk – knows something we don't?

FIB Nick Cave was born with a tail, which he later had surgically removed.

FACT Although widely reported as a sensational rock fact for years, this was the famously laugh-loving Australian's idea of a joke.

FIB Alan McGee: 'There was this band called TV Personalities… I couldn't believe anyone could be this mental (when I saw them live)… it was just insane… the next day I went to Rough Trade and stole all their records.' (Quote from *Upside Down: The Creation Records Story*.)

FACT As anyone who has ever attempted to shoplift vinyl records can confirm, the would-be thief's work is cut out by the universal practice of record shops only displaying the sleeves of the records on the shop floor, keeping the products inside them behind the counter. So how did McGee accomplish this audacious crime? Did he con his way behind the counter and then manage to carefully pick out each of the band's records before shoving the resulting collection of albums and singles under his jacket? Answers on a half-inched record sleeve please.

FIB Primal Scream were banned from the BBC's *Top of the Pops* show after turning down a gig because they would have to fly into Luton Airport, which was 'not rock'n'roll enough'.

FACT Bobby Gillespie later explained this story in an April 2006 interview with *NME*. He claimed it came from a press statement by the band's management as the result of a band in-joke: 'Me and Andrew Innes have always said "We can't go near Luton; it would be terrible if we crashed at Luton Airport or if the last gig was there. It's not right, is it? It's not mythical. It's not legendary. We were on tour in Dublin and then we were going to play Cork and they wanted us to fly from Dublin to Luton, spend an day at *Top Of The Pops*, which involves hanging about for nine hours, fly to Cork and miss the soundcheck and do the gig. And we decided, You know what? Let's just get on the bus and go to Cork. We thought it was a waste of a day. I don't think we were ever banned from *Top Of The Pops*." '

FIB   Primal Scream keyboard player Martin Duffy was stabbed in New York – without realising.

FACT   In July 1993 the man known to his band mates simply as 'Duffy' was slumped in a New York bar when a member of staff pointed out that he was bleeding heavily and looked like he might have been shot. It was later found that his backside had been pierced by a sharp implement; he was rushed to hospital to get stitched up, and the story was duly spread to the music press that the ever-adventurous piano-fondler had been stabbed by an anonymous assailant. It was only a few years later that it was established that he had sustained his injuries by falling from a bookcase onto a table full of glasses.

FIB   Rapper Akon served three years in prison between 1999 and 2002 as the 'ringleader of a notorious car theft operation,' 'fought almost every day for two years,' and wrote early hit 'Locked Up' about his experiences while incarcerated.

FACT   As an exposé by the US website *The Smoking Gun* revealed in 2008, although he had spent a few months in jail awaiting trial after his arrest on suspicion of stealing a BMW in 1998 (the charges were later dropped), and has several other arrests on his rap sheet, the man born Aliaune Damala Badara Thiam has but one solitary felony conviction to his name. That was for gun possession, for which he received three years probation, not prison. Akon's tales of 'facing 75 years,' being grassed up by jealous gang underlings and constant fights in the clink, not to mention his claim of having written 'Locked Up' in there, were repeated continually, but have been shown to be not just untrue, but also suspiciously similar to the plotline of the Nicolas Cage movie *Gone In 60 Seconds*.

Akon's reaction to these accusations? 'To focus and put energy on negative things like that, to try to discredit an artist, it makes no sense to me.' Dwelling on negative stuff – what kind of prison-obsessed, crime-glorifying fool would want to do that, eh?

FIB The Manic Street Preachers promised to split up after one, million-selling double album.

FACT Well, one out of three ain't too bad. *Generation Terrorists* was a double album, but it sold only around a quarter of the magic million mark. As for splitting up, well, as of 2011 the Manics were promoting *National Treasures*, their greatest hits collection, after a career spanning a further two decades. Can you ever forgive them?

FIB Sandi Thom's basement webcam 'gigs' generated 100,000 viewers through word of mouth.

FACT Considerable doubt has been cast upon the then 'unknown' Scottish singer-songwriter's claim that her '21 Nights From Tooting' series of webcam gigs from her South London basement in 2006 began with 60 views and miraculously multiplied to upwards of 100,000 hits, through the pure and simple power of song, aided and abetted by word of mouth. Soon after she received a torrent of publicity for her innovative 'tour' it was noted that she had Beyonce Knowles' management, a lucrative publishing deal and a PR company behind her, and that the upsurge in web traffic only transpired once her 'success story' had been featured in the papers.

But let's not judge her too harshly. Creating your own publicity is an art in itself, so if her only crime is to have manipulated the media a little, I say good luck to the lass. Actually, on second thoughts, I've just had a listen to her smash hit debut single, 'I Wish I Were A Punk Rocker (With Flowers In My Hair)'. Hello, is that the fraud squad?!

FIB   The Beastie Boys' funded their debut album with the proceeds of an early b-side which was sampled on a British Airways ad; they recorded *Paul's Boutique* in the original Batcave from the '60s TV series; they make bespoke digital watches.

FACT   The Beastie Boys are compulsive liars. And God bless them for it.

FIB   The Aphex Twin claimed variously: he didn't sleep for a month; he recorded the *Drukqs* in the bath; he's deaf; that Radiohead pay him 70 per cent of the royalties from their *Kid A* album, such is his influence on it; that he worked as a tin miner at 17 to finance his early career, where 'It's really hot underground and miners walk around with either pants or with a belt on and nothing else. I was well spun out.'

FACT   I cannot conclusively disprove any of the above.

FIB   Diana Ross discovered the Jacksons.

FACT   From their earliest days as Motown recording artists, official biographies of the all-singing, all-dancing family from Gary, Indiana informed us that the five boys had been discovered by former Supremes star Diana Ross, performing at a charity gig for the Mayor of Gary in 1969. Their ages were also changed, with Michael listed as only nine years old (rather than his real age of 11) to make him appear cuter. In fact Motown had been monitoring the band since two years before, on the recommendation of other soul acts such as Sam & Dave and Gladys Knight. That didn't stop Motown boss Berry Gordy from entitling their debut album *Diana Ross Presents The Jackson Five*, and instructing all other acts on the label to back up the story of how they were signed.

Despite this fairy story, it didn't do them any harm, as their debut single, 'I Want You Back', went to number one a mere five months after their first Ross-endorsed live appearance. Nonetheless, the Jacksons always resented the suggestion that they didn't make it big by themselves, and as recently as September 2011 Jermaine Jackson was heard fuming about this fictional story in an interview with *The Times*. Let it go, Jerm, let it go.

SOME MIGHT SAY

DUMB AND DUMBER

'I know it's a very flippant thing to say, but if Kurt Cobain
had played football, he'd probably be alive today.'

Damon Albarn, 1995

'We have this thing in the band. It's like being blood
brothers. Today, I saw this pool of elephant piss. I stuck my
finger in and licked it, so all the others had to do the same.
So we're now elephant's piss brothers as well...'

Paul Heaton, The Beautiful South, 1994

'The Internet's completely over. I don't see why I should
give my new music to iTunes or anyone else. They won't
pay me an advance for it and then they get angry when
they can't get it.'

Prince, 2010

*That's fine, Prince. But I feel duty bound to point out that you've got to
give it to someone, or nobody will ever hear it.*

'Osama bin Laden is the only one who knows exactly what
I'm going through.'

**R. Kelly on his prosecution for filming himself
having sex with an underage girl, 2003**

'Wave will hit 8am them crazy white boys going to try to go surfing,'

50 Cent reacting on Twitter to the Japanese tsunami, 2011

'Up 20 places in the US charts, it's been a great week for Roy Orbison.'

Gary Davies, Radio One, 1989

Orbison died in December 1988.

'She's weird as f**k. Who knows, she might have a snake or a knife in her pussy if you try to get some from her.

Snoop Dogg on Lady Gaga, 2011

'My broken foot has given me a new respect for people who don't have legs.'

Jessie J, 2011

'How did you all meet?'

Presenter Donna Air to The Corrs, MTV, late 1990s

'The Rolling Stones suffered a great loss with the death of Ian Stewart, the man who had for so many years played piano and quietly and silently with them on stage.'

Andy Peebles, Radio One, 1986

We rock hacks are often criticised for an overly negative attitude towards music. Yet if you flick through the reviews pages of any given music magazine, you will find that around 90 per cent of reviews are broadly positive.

No, really. If you don't believe me, have a flick through and see how many are marked at least 3 out of 5 or 6 out of 10.

We're also as guilty of getting wildly over-excited about music as any screaming boy band fan. And that's no bad thing. Pop music's job is primarily to get you wildly over-excited. Better to reflect that feeling and look a bit of a berk a year later than report on it like it was an interesting fluctuation in the Japanese bond markets.

So get wildly over-excited I did, drunk as a fruit fly on the head-swimming harvestof Britpop as it stormed the charts in the summer of 1995. Reviewing Blur's disappointingly patchy, overly theatrical third album *The Great Escape*, I didn't pull any plaudits...

DON'T BELIEVE the hYPe 7.

WILD PRAISE AND PURPLE PROSE

'An album which, even in the wake of a run of exceptional albums by British bands, sets a new standard for British guitar pop in the '90s... it's utterly beyond contemporary compare.'

Blur, *The Great Escape*, reviewed by Johnny Cigarettes, *NME*,9 September 1995

And I wasn't alone. Here's a selection of other soundbites:

'A truly great pop record.'

The Times

'It is the most truthful mirror modern pop has yet held up to '90s Britain.'

The Observer

'The benchmark against which all other British pop bands must be measured.'

The Independent On Sunday

'Will put them amongst true pop greats... Oasis, do your worst.'

The Sunday Times

Buried in the midst of my NME review of that album, however, are the misgivings which I should perhaps have given more consideration to. Reading it back, I can see exactly the qualifying paragraph where that unease was unwisely buried. So I have taken the liberty of editing my words from that paragraph to right the wrongs of history:

'It falls ~~just~~ WAY short of being a masterpiece. There are undeniable weaknesses: the ~~slightly~~ VERY restrictive third person lyrical approach; the obsession with ~~mildly~~ HIGHLY anachronistic sit-com caricatures; the cultural tourist attraction to a rubbish modern lifestyle that Damon doesn't ~~always~~ know ~~that well~~ ANYTHING ABOUT; the ~~vague~~ OBVIOUS filler quality of ~~a couple~~ THE MAJORITY of tunes; the continuing ~~mischievous~~ IRRITATING affection for frivolous, flimsy muso-kitsch.'

And piss-weak tunes, I forgot to mention piss-weak tunes.

Anyway, I'm still working through it with my therapist, and this is all an important part of coming to terms with my past misdemeanours.

In contrast to the magic mushroom cloud of hyperbole that formed around the above release, the Oasis album released just three weeks later was greeted with decidedly lukewarm reviews (One of which is featured on page 12).

Over the months that followed, however, Oasis's stock rose to the point where that summer was ubiquitously soundtracked by the Sun-shee-ine sounds of the Gallagher brothers and their band of not particularly merry waxworks in casual rainwear. And the more we found ourselves unable to escape Morning Glory, *the more it dawned on the doubters that it had a damn sight more going for it than Blur's effort.*

Those were heady days, of course, and it was easy to get carried away with the prevailing tide of opinion as we rode on the crest of a wave of optimism surrounding 'Cool Britannia' and all who sailed in her. (Liking the extended metaphor? Thanks. In keeping with the spirit of the times to which I refer, I've just had a quick line of some top quality bugle and, reading it back, I realise IT ROCKS BELLS AND I AM THE KING OF THE WORLD. Now get out of my way.)

By 1997, any doubts about the Gallagher brothers' godlike status had been comprehensively banished from polite society. So when their third album, Be Here Now *was released in August 1997, the torrent of praise could have floated Noah's ark.*

Here is a selection of the notices that greeted it:

'*Be Here Now* is a triumph. It is also the album that will make Oasis into a global force, insinuating itself into tormented, hopeful young hearts from Indiana to Jakarta and filling arenas full of waving scarves and flaming cigarette lighters across the planet.'

Neil Spencer, review on the front page, *The Observer*

'Huge as a planet, *Be Here Now* rolls as slowly as a planet also, and just as unstoppably. You have to go back to efforts like The Beatles' *Revolver* for a set whose every constituent could be spun off into the singles chart.'

Paul Du Noyer, *Q*

'This is the Oasis world domination album. Dem a come fe mess up de area seeeeeerious.'

Charles Shaar Murray, *Mojo*

Jah, dem no it Charles. And so it was that those cuttings take their place among a proud tradition of hyperbole far beyond the call of duty. Because the art of overstatement is a noble one, as the following collection of misplaced predictions, delirious description and drooling hyperbole will demonstrate.

Some of these reviews are about perfectly decent music, but all of them have let their euphoria get the better of them. And, like moonwalking naked on a table at a family gathering – it's amusing, entirely forgivable, but not altogether appropriate…

'I really think The Incredible String Band will rule the world in a year's time. Their sound is so intricate and delicate, like an exquisite tapestry.'

John Peel, presenter of Radio One's *Top Gear* ('a bastion of hip sounds in a world of relentless commerciality'), reviewing the singles in *Melody Maker*, 30 March, 1968

Just imagine readers, a world in which The Incredible String Band ruled…

'Jobriath is going to be the biggest artist in the world. He is a singer, dancer, woman, man. He has the glamour of Garbo. He is beautiful.'

Jerry Brandt (Jobriath's manager), *Melody Maker, 12 January* 1974

'HIPSWAY: BORN TO BE KING'

NME cover headline, April 1986

They didn't have another hit

'Sensibilities are deflowered, blood boils, bowels split, my dusty copy of 'Mystery Train' combusts spontaneously in my hand… The world (represented by a mere 23 people tonight) lay down and let itself be trampled on. I hollered for more 'til my throat bled, then dragged my carcass home to find my entire record collection fused into a single molten blob of vinyl. The most exciting show I've ever EVER seen, ever. Where were you?!?'

World Domination Enterprises, reviewed live at The Underground, Croydon, Simon Reynolds, _Melody Maker_, January 1987

'James Maker will one day be so famous that he'll be *totally* unbearable. And if there have to be rock gods, we should be thankful that he will be one of them.'

Raymonde, _Babelogue_, reviewed by Myrna Minkoff, _NME_, 17 October, 1987

'They make you try harder, but then you really defy gravity, that's the joy. I mean it's like gravity comes along and you smirk and whip out a cutlass. Southampton I hardly knew you: I was somewhere above the moon, which was full of itself. Infinity for breakfast.'

Throwing Muses, reviewed live at Southampton University, by Chris Roberts, _Melody Maker_, 1 July, 1989

'FIRST THINGS first, l*t's wip* out out all th* *'s. Th*r*'s too many drugs in NM* alr*ady. And anyway Happy Mondays hav* just chann*ll*d a hundr*d w*ight of th*m into th* Haci*nda's PA and now th*y'r* all playing havoc with th* sound syst*m."

**Happy Mondays r*vi*w*d liv* at Manch*st*r Haci*nda, by H*l*n M*ad,
*NM**, May 20, 1989**

*Can you s** what sh*'s don* th*r*, r*ad*rs?*
*And how many lin*s did you manag* b*for* your h*ad hurt?*

'There's no reason why they shouldn't be a further stepping stone on the journey to a perfect punkpopdance amalgam. Right now they're halfway to paradise with youth, spirit and time on their side. Shall we take a trip?'

Northside, reviewed live by Bob Stanley, *Melody Maker*, 6 Jan 1990

Er, sorry Bob, I can't. I've got to help my mum round Tesco's…

'Berenyi is androgynous in the true sense of the word; male and female incarnate and carnal, an erotic, mysterious other. Everything flows from him, and halfway through they reach melting point. Then they begin to steam.

Suddenly, their latent energy blossoms, and it feels like every muscle is being bathed in fire, red hot mercury licking your veins until every nerve-ending starts to overload, disappearing into the ecstasy of its own glow…Under Neath What give new meaning to the term, "go f*** yourself".

**Under Neath What, reviewed live by Jonathan Selzer,
Melody Maker, 19 January 1991**

'If Marc Bolan were alive today, he'd be in Altern 8.'

**Stuart Maconie, giving joint single of the week to Isotonik, 'Different Strokes'
and LFO,'What Is House', *NME*, 4 January 1992**

'Pop is rarely so frothing and rarely less frothy…as exciting as white water rafting down the river Styx. Fame? Not 'If', when.'

Scorpio Rising, *If*, reviewed by John Mulvey, *NME*, 4 January 1992

'To hear Young Gods is to be cleansed, purged, purified, ennobled. To feel the first stirrings of the Nietzschian superman in your soul. Be not afraid.'

Young Gods, reviewed live by Simon Price, *Melody Maker*, 22 February, 1992

'A Robert Johnson for the nineties.'

Daniel Johnston profiled by Everett True, *Melody Maker*, 4 April 1992

I presume this is a bespectacled, tone-deaf indie milque-toast Robert Johnson he refers to, not some growling, hellhound-pursued blues pioneer…

'Right Said Fred are the sort of band who make the kind of music ABC and the Human League were always too busy talking about making to actually do… one day Right Said Fred will be bigger than Prince, Madonna, Michael Jackson and even Blur. (8/10)

Right Said Fred, *Up*, reviewed by David Quantick, *NME*, 9 May 1992

'Fashion spreads will fall at its feet. West London style-victims will mull over its intricacies while supping bottled beers in Soho brasseries. Clothes designers will flood the catwalks with v-necks and shrink fit trousers.'

Feature on 'The New Wave of New Wave', by John Harris and Paul Moody, *NME*, 8 January 1994

'Suddenly, they're here. A crackle of white light, a rumbling sonic current, and Ian lollops to the mike to say... "Ay oop!"

A few seconds dramatic pause follows, and then there's a bassline. Oh... Lord... yes, it's "I Wanna be Adored", and the sheer ecstasy is impossible to describe. Hearing that beautiful, crystalline guitar pattern kissing the sky above you after five or six years of loving and hoping in your bedroom... people are on the brink of tears. Honestly.

But it's John Squire who is the Grand Vizier of this mysterious star chamber. Silently all-powerful, sprinkling madly sublime magic over the scene, he just cannot fail. Mani is all vibes, thrusting his aquaplaning bass undercurrents teasingly at us... And Ian, dripping hard-eyed arrogance, unimpeachably mythical, strokes a tambourine and croons pure honey and poison.'

The Stone Roses, reviewed live at Feile festival, Ireland, Johnny Cigarettes, *NME*, 1995

What can I say – I was quite excited. And the drummer from Dodgy had given me half an 'E'.

'Britpop, having served its purpose, has just been executed. This is a revolution. Boys and girls, introducing ROMO, pop's newest flash dash into style, glamour, romance and the excitement of fashion and synthetic culture.'

***Melody Maker*'s 'Romo' special issue from 25 November, 1995**

… featuring future superstars such as Orlando, Minty, Viva, Hollywood, Plastic Fantastic, Sextus, and Dexdexter.

'The new renaissance painters of pop, loading their palette with every musical colour and texture from Dexy's and Funkadelic to Kraftwerk and The Vapors. Van Gogh cut off his ear not for art, but because he'd never live to hear Octopus.'

Octopus, tips for 1996, Dave Simpson, *Melody Maker,* 6 January 1996

'When we dream of Noel, we touch the limits of what we aspire to and what we also balk at becoming. Gallagher is a dream-creature to be both worshipped and worried about.'

Emma Forrest on Oasis, *The Independent,* March 1996

'Completely, absolutely, gobsmackingly dazzling. This, people, is Mozart at the wheel of a monster truck. It's an earthquake directed by the Coen brothers. It is pure pleasure siphoned from the adrenal gland and shot into the cerebral cortex through a titanium syringe… It is Fat Of The Land, the album that ate the world … it will blow your mind and grind the pieces into the carpet under its size 14 boots.'

The Prodigy, *The Fat Of The Land*, reviewed by David Bennun, *The Guardian,* June 1997

'Christ almighty. It moves vertically through salted pressures with a head that can see sideways. It is red in tooth and claw. It swoons and burns and swells and cracks and froths at the mouth… It is shattering the atmosphere. It glows from every burst pore. It is a tormenting wind murmuring. It is a curious germination. It is pleasure playing a tenchant and mystic melody on the sharp edge of a thin dream.'

The Prodigy, *The Fat Of The Land*, reviewed by Paul Morley, *Uncut*, July 1997

It's not bad.

'The guitars are a fluctuating matrix for intangible Verlainian energies, the guitars are guitars in the way that guitars are guitars and sometimes they're not.'

Radiohead, *OK Computer*, reviewed by Paul Morley, *Uncut*, July 1997

'Only one band want to make records that blow holes through the limits of what we currently meekly accept as sonically reasonable in the field of rock. Only one band can. And that's Terris.'

**Terris, 'The first new stars of 2000', profiled by Ted Kessler,
NME, 15 January 2000**

'This is brilliant! What if Steps didn't eagerly suck pus from a maggot-infested and hideously noisome festering sore situated halfway between Satan's spike-studded scrotal sac and his gnashing teeth-filled anal crack, hmmm? Then they'd sound exactly like Scooch.... it rules like Genghis Khan ruled – remorselessly, frighteningly, tyrannically but absolutely irresistibly. Love it. Fear it. Worship it. Obey it. Or DIE!'

**Scooch, 'More Than I Needed To Know' (single)
reviewed by Steven Wells, *NME*, 15 January , 2000**

'Radiohead have pushed their rock trolley out into deep space and come back with something so complex it makes the hieroglyphics on the pyramids look like graffiti on a bus stop... Radiohead have constructed a crazy intergalactic rock coracle out of the Difficult Jazz Things section at HMV and they're rowing it to Mars.'

Radiohead, *Kid A*, reviewed by Caitlin Moran, *The Times*, July 2000

BIGGER THAN JESUS!
ANDREW WK
MEET THE SAVIOUR OF MUSIC

***NME* cover, 2001**
Actually, erm, the saviour will be along in a minute. In the meantime, here's some berk with red felt tip on his face.

'Like Prometheus chained to his rock, the eagle eating his liver out night after night, Kylie becomes Love's sacrificial lamb, bleating an earnest invitation to the drooling, ravenous wolf to devour her time and time again, all to a groovy techno beat. "I'll take you back, I'll take you back again." Indeed, here the love song becomes a vehicle for a harrowing portrait of humanity, not dissimilar to the Old Testament psalms. Both are messages to God that cry out into the yawning void, in anguish and self-loathing, for deliverance.'

Kylie Minogue, 'Better The Devil You Know' (single), appraised by Nick Cave,
***The Guardian*, May 2001**

'Fischerspooner are the best thing to happen to music since electricity. This is a new beginning for pop music. We will never have to be bored again. Fischerspooner are the first band to give you more than everything you always wanted.'

Fischerspooner feature from '2002 – The New Batch', Gavin McInnes,
***NME*, 5 January 2002**

'In its own subtle way, 'White Christmas' is a musical gesture as aggressive as 'Anarchy In The UK' or anything on Eminem's *The Marshall Mathers LP*. Listening to the song's lulling, maudlin, immemorial strains, we hear something more than a seasonal standard; the toughest punk anthem ever to masquerade as a Christmas carol.'

Judy Rosen, *The Observer*, December 2002

'It's not really about music. He's more an instinctive psychosexual performance poet and, arguably, one of the finest socio-political commentators America ever had.'

Marilyn Manson, interviewed by Barbara Ellen,
***The Observer* magazine, May 2003**

'Art/punk duo Selfish Cunt aren't simply an in-joke… more a malignancy at the heart of the fashionable life… genuinely menacing double A-side 'Britain Is Shit/F**k The Poor' is the most brutal state-of-the-nation address since the Sex Pistols' 'God Save The Queen'.'

'The best 40 bands in Britain', *The Guardian*, September 2003

'New rave; a rebirth of punk flying alongside the soul of dance music and under the influence of lost weekends on interstellar Ketamine terror-cruises.'

Klaxons, *Myths of the Near Future*, reviewed by Alex Miller, *NME*, 27 January, 2006

'As a club DJ I rock bangers that create crazy excitement in the party. The original was a hood classic – so big they made me a 'special' – a revoiced version dedicated to me. Shit is straight banging, ATL trap music meets JA shottas. It's an ugly situation.'

Young Jeezy & Akon, 'Soul Survivor (The Gun Session remix)', reviewed in 'The Last Track I Loved', Q, May 2006

'She stretched time and space until they snapped, slinging the concept of the genre in the cosmos to be gorged on by a trio of luminescent hip-hop phoenixes'.

MIA, *Kala*, reviewed by Alex Miller, *NME*, 11 August, 2006

Finally, no feature on misplaced hype could be complete without mentioning the legendary review of John Lennon and Yoko Ono's Wedding Album from 1969 that appeared in Melody Maker shortly before its release. The album features a single track on side one entitled simply 'John & Yoko', in which the pair's heartbeats are the backdrop for a 25-minute recording of the couple calling out to each other in various 'emotional' states, from fear to affection.

Side two's only track 'Amsterdam' featured interview snippets with the couple from their 'bed in' and incidental background noise.

However, when preview copies of the album were sent out prior to release, the two recordings were pressed as two single-sided LPs with only a test signal on the two blank sides. That didn't deter Melody Maker's Richard Williams from reviewing it in full, presuming this was a full, four-sided double album. He reported:

'Sides Two and Four consist entirely of single tones maintained throughout, presumably produced electronically. This might sound arid, to say the least, but in fact constant listening reveals a curious point: the pitch of the tones alters frequently, but only by micro-tones or, at most, a semi-tone. This oscillation produces an almost subliminal, uneven 'beat' which maintains interest.'

He concludes: 'This album will make interesting listening in 20 years' time. What will we think of us then?'

A week later he received a telegram from John and Yoko which read:

'DEAR RICHARD THANK YOU FOR YOUR FANTASTIC REVIEW ON OUR WEDDING ALBUM INCLUDING C-AND-D SIDE STOP WE ARE CONSIDERING IT FOR OUR NEXT RELEASE STOP MAYBE YOU ARE RIGHT IN SAYING THAT THEY ARE THE BEST SIDES STOP WE BOTH FEEL THAT THIS IS THE FIRST TIME A CRITIC TOPPED THE ARTIST STOP WE ARE NOT JOKING STOP LOVE AND PEACE STOP JOHN AND YOKO LENNON."

SOME MIGHT SAY

THE DRUGS DO WORK

'I'm extremely careful. I've never turned blue in someone else's bathroom. I consider that the height of bad manners. I've had so many people do it to me and it's really not on.'

Keith Richards, 1978

'I was a drug addict, so my insides are fine. My liver's a bit hard but all the damage that's been done to me is really by drugs, and that can be repaired.'

Shaun Ryder, 1992

This is the man who has conducted many an interview while scoffing Rennie by the packet. Would you want to be inside his body?

'Speed for breakfast, speed for lunch and a square meal in the evening.'

These Animal Men motto, 1994

'There's nothing wrong with drugs as long as you use and don't abuse. Like, I wouldn't shoot up drugs while I was drunk…'

Kim Deal, 1994

'I'm careful about how much I do. I wouldn't go to a rave and take six E's without drinking water.'

Elastica's Donna Matthews, 1995

'Every few weeks I have a day when I just take mushrooms, without eating or drinking, and it really clears my head.'

Tricky, 1996

'I snorted my father. He was cremated and I couldn't resist – it went down pretty well.'

Keith Richards, 2007

'I spent my 16th birthday high as a kite jumping out of a tree topless in my local park just because it felt amazing hitting the ground.'

Florence Welch, 2009

Was that the whole day Florence? How many times did you do this? What did the local tramps make of it all? How high was the tree? Not saying you're exaggerating or anything, but, you know…

'There's a rumour I was doing 50 rocks (of crack) a day and that each rock contained 20 grams of coke, so I'd be doing 600 grammes a day. That's rubbish. I think I was only smoking about 15 or 20 rocks a day.'

Shaun Ryder, 1992

There comes a time in every musician's life when they must explore more weighty matters than midweek chart positions and covering groupies in lemon curd. That is when they invariably turn to a higher power for the answers they seek.

But far be it from these independently minded souls to rely on the conventional faiths they might find by walking into their nearest place of worship. Rare is the instance of successful rock stars setting foot in the impossibly square, all-too-familiar territory of conventional Christianity, be it Anglican, Roman Catholic or Seventh Day Adventist. No, your true rock'n'roll renegade seeks a more exotic flavour of faith.

Yet the further afield they look, the sillier the philosophies seem to become. And somehow none of the belief systems practised seem to sit very comfortably with the tradition of unbridled free expression that popular music holds dear. In this chapter we look at just some of the more popular belief systems most closely associated with the devil's music...

hallelujah!

8.

ROCK'N'ROLL'S DAFTEST RELIGIONS

Rastafarianism

Within tolerant, multi-cultural liberal circles here in the west, it is considered rather taboo to have anything but 'respect' for religions of all stripes, even if their doctrines revolve around the notion of a shady cabal of 9,000-year-old Duck-billed Platypuses being the true rulers of the world.

Nowhere is this more true than with the followers of Rastafari. It is exceptionally rare to hear anyone voice so much as a squeak of scepticism as to the frankly barmy set of beliefs entertained by more than a million people worldwide. I mean, sure, its followers have made some top tunes, but does that make their beliefs beyond reproach?

This, remember, is a religion based on one central tenet: Emperor Haile Selassie I of Ethiopia (1892–1975) is a living God. Yes, that's right, not just your average, here-today-gone-tomorrow God. Not the kind of God that might succumb to pancreatic cancer or choke on a chicken bone, but a living, looking-increasingly-immortal God.

But even if we dismiss the widespread belief that his death in 1975 was a hoax, as Gods go, you'd have to say that Selassie didn't show a huge amount of omnipotence, omniscience, or indeed beneficence during the 44 years he held his earthly political office.

Admittedly, it was under his watch that slavery was finally abolished in Ethiopia, although that was only after Italian occupying forces had put a stop to it in 1935 (imagine having Mussolini's fascists lecturing you on human rights) and pressure from the allies during the Second World War. So it took him 12 years of his reign to finally pass a law abolishing a practice that all but three other countries in the world had done away with.

During that time, far from being embraced as the 'black Christ' that rastas revere, he wasn't making that many friends among his countrymen. Indeed, another rasta hero who the bredren often praise in the same breath, the black nationalist and 'prophet' Marcus Garvey, condemned him as 'a great coward' for 'surrendering himself to the white wolves of Europe,' when he fled to Europe during the Italian invasion. When the prophet condemns the God, you've surely got problems…

But these are really the least of the crimes that can be laid at Selassie's door.

Human Rights Watch records Selassie's misrule of the north of the country thus:

'In 1974, the Emperor Haile Selassie became notorious for his attempts to conceal the existence of the famine of 1972–73 in Wollo. This, however, was only one in a succession of such incidents. Prof. Mesfin Wolde Mariam of Addis Ababa University has documented how the famines of 1958 and 1966 in Tigray and Wollo were treated with official indifference, bordering on hostility towards the peasants who were considered sufficiently ungrateful for the divinely-sanctioned rule of Haile Selassie as to allow themselves to defame his reputation by dying of famine.'

The result was that around 100,000 people died of starvation under his watch.

But whether or not he was the messiah or just a naughty boy, the origins of this religion have arguably less bearing on the modern world than the social customs set in stone by them.

Women in particular get a raw deal. Forbidden from being leaders, they are basically there as housekeepers and childbearers. Menstruating women are not allowed to prepare food, and they are forbidden from wearing make-up or revealing clothing, as that is tantamount to promiscuity. Still, at least these days the dreadlocked Taliban are just about OK with the concept of women being educated.

More worryingly, birth control is also forbidden as a European tactic to suppress the development of the African population. And if you get pregnant? Sorry, abortion is a strict no-no. What if we catch HIV? Can't imagine old Haile rising from the dead to offer any wisdom…

And if you think turning to your own sex might help, you're sorely mistaken. As gays and lesbians throughout the Caribbean are viciously persecuted and frequently murdered due to their sexuality, there's no hope of Rastafari demonstrating their much-documented empathy with persecuted minorities, and coming to the rescue any time soon – for them, homosexuality has always been a mortal sin in the eyes of 'Jah'.

And as for racism, well, rasta heroes like Garvey didn't mince their words when advocating separation of races and the superiority of black people.

If these were the policies of a political party, they'd share more ideology with the BNP than the liberal-minded folk that are often attracted to Rastafari's more cuddly cultural accoutrements.

But they call it a religion, so have some respect and pass the dutchie if you don't mind awfully…

Kabbalah

The practice of drinking your own pee would probably have remained mercifully outside the public consciousness had actress Sarah Miles not made herself (in)famous for publicly endorsing it. Likewise, this esoteric, astrology-based offshoot of Judaism would probably have remained within the realm of the rich, gullible but relatively anonymous if Madonna hadn't started singing its praises.

Ms Ciccone might seem an unlikely convert, given her highly liberated attitude to sexuality – something that she has never been slow to criticise Catholicism for repressing. Among the beliefs propounded by the Kabbalah philosophy (they prefer not to be known as a 'religion'), is a set of rules regarding the beast with two backs which you'd imagine the woman who wrote 'Erotica' might have found a little distasteful.

Kabbalah's basic 'philosophy' is all based around the somewhat hazy notion of maximising 'Light', the nebulous group of energies that flow between humans, which can be coaxed out of us through meditation and 'shared consciousness'.

Among their beliefs is the edict that a couple should not engage in sex with the woman positioned above the man, as she is then drawing energies into herself from below, instead of above. Well, if you insist…

Furthermore, when a woman's insides come into contact with a man's sperm, they are interacting with the essence of their energy and are affected by this for several years. Surely a routine visit to your local clap clinic could solve that?

Another instruction is that the man should not orgasm before the woman, as it injects selfishness into the act of love-making. But what if, as Loudon Wainwright III once protested, 'You used to say I came too early… but it was you who came too late'?

Meanwhile, the most 'Light' is derived from sex that occurs early Saturday morning. So not content with all your other restrictions on simple sensual pleasures, now you want us to interrupt our weekend lie-in? Sadists.

And in case all that self-repression might tempt you into a little discreet personal relief, you should also bear in mind that men are forbidden from masturbating, as the discarded sperm are abandoned souls that become demons. A worrying thought, since I alone must have released enough demons as a teenager to populate Hades several times over.

All this is fairly harmless superstition, you might argue. But a 2005 BBC documentary found some more disturbing practices in operation when visiting the London Kabbalah Centre. An undercover reporter who visited their £3.7million building off Oxford Street, seeking help to cure the cancer he was suffering from, was offered a package of remedies for the disease for £860 – nearly £400 for 10 cases of Kabbalah water, £150 for 'extra-strength' water and £289 for Zohar books – the Kabbalah 'bible'.

The water was traced back to a bottling plant in Ontario, Canada.

Still, Madonna allegedly has it in her central heating system, so next time you get a bout of flu, maybe just loiter around outside her security gates and you might catch a few revitalising 'energies'.

However, now Guy has flown the coop, she might struggle to benefit fully, since in the Kabbalah the men wear white because, as one believer put it, 'they are the ones reaching the light through prayer, while women are only vessels.'

Oh, and then there's Eliyahu Yardeni, a senior figure at the London centre who had given lectures to Madonna, Demi Moore and others, who explained away the holocaust by saying, 'Just to tell you another thing about the six million Jews that were killed in the Holocaust: the question was that the Light was blocked. They didn't use Kabbalah.'

Wow, 60 years of searching for reasons why, and this guy nails it. And guess what? It was all their own fault!

So what was it that brought the megalomaniacal multi-millionaire Madonna and this strange bunch of cults together? 'The thought of eternal life appeals to me,' Madonna said of the religion. 'I don't think people's energy just disappears.'

Immortality – what self-respecting pop star wouldn't aspire to that?

Hinduism and Hare Krishna

George Harrison's celebrated Beatles song, 'Taxman' sees our hero angrily decrying the inland revenue for taking such a large cut of his millions to pay for trivial luxuries like hospitals, schools and housing.

That might seem a touch uncharitable, but perhaps we should consider it in the context of his wider framework of beliefs. After all, he was already becoming a keen follower of the Hindu faith, and he may well have felt he did something right in a past life to be rewarded with the talent and success he enjoyed from a very young age. And as for the rest of the poor saps who he has to pay taxes to keep from starvation, well, they must have run over a kitten in a previous life – that's the Hindu way of looking at it, at any rate.

Karma is a word often mentioned in artistic circles as a warm, cuddly, hippy kinda concept. One which rewards benevolent behaviour and promotes peace, love and understanding. And in some ways, that's true. But it also has a more punitive meaning, particularly in Hinduism. And like much religious dogma, it conveniently reinforces and morally validates the social, political and economic status quo.

If, for instance, you are born disabled or dirt poor, Hindu teachings have it that this must be the result of crimes committed in a past life. Some argue that this is part of the reason why the afflicted and destitute are often disregarded in Hindu countries and the rigid caste system is so entrenched.

The benefit of Karma, supposedly, is that the disadvantaged person will ask 'Why me?' and will then learn the lesson that they must strive for a better future. Who knows, maybe if they're really, really good, they'll end up reborn as a millionaire womanising hypocrite like George Harrison?

Harrison was a prominent cheerleader for a highly distinctive strand of Hinduism originally known as Krishnaism, a faith embodied since the 1960s by the International Society For Krishna Consciousness (ISKCON), known to us unbelievers as Hare Krishna devotees.

Although, like Harrison, relatively few musicians have been sufficiently moved to reach for the head shaver and dig out an orange bedsheet from the airing cupboard, Hare Krishna has always been given highly respectful props in pop circles.

Meanwhile, the movement's rejection of material possessions and meat-eating has helped it cultivate an image of a laid back, peace-loving, free thinking alternative lifestyle.

Yet the actual teachings of Hare Krishna figures such as founder A.C. Bhaktivedanta Swami Prabhupada are a touch less easy-going. He preached the rejection of physical pleasures such as the eating of fish, meat or eggs; the use of intoxicants such as marijuana, illicit sex, and gambling and frivolous sports, are called the four regulative principles.

Meanwhile, music might be allowed, but you'd be expected to devote much of it to holy songs. Elevation and joy are to be derived from chanting God's holy names, while your guitar gently weeps due to its newly unemployed status.

Even our George failed pretty miserably to live up to the standards of behaviour he preached. 'I hope to get out of this place by the Lord Sri Krishna's grace,' he sang on 'Living In The Material World', 'My salvation from the material world.'

That didn't stop him dabbling in his fair share of cocaine, illicit sex, smoking and drinking. Which is no reason to crucify the guy. That would be rather harsh. But you do fear for his Karma, a notion which Krishna endorses in the same way as its related creed of Hinduism. Might George end up a more modest figure in the next life? A binman perhaps, or, Krishna forfend, a tax inspector?

Nation of Islam

'A follower of Farrakhan,' proclaimed Public Enemy's Chuck D on 'Don't Believe The Hype'. 'Don't tell me that you understand, until you hear the man.'

Well, I have heard the man, and read a fair bit about him and his organisation Nation of Islam, and it's certainly not too hard to understand what Chuck and many other black artists have liked about an ideology that claims black people are the original race of humans, direct descendents of Abraham, and effectively God's chosen people.

But looking a little further into the beliefs propagated by NOI, it takes some pretty energetic leaps of faith to take them seriously at all.

There is no point in inventing a religion unless you declare yourself the messiah, and that's what the rather shady figure of Wallace Fard Muhammad (aka a New Zealand-born petty criminal called Wallace Dodd Ford, according to the FBI, but they have been known to make up porkies to discredit radical groups) did when he founded Nation of Islam in 1930. Or at least, his successor Elijah Muhammad awarded him that title when W. Fard Muhammad disappeared without trace in June 1934.

The scant evidence for the latter's whereabouts was ultimately accounted for by the Nation Of Islam's explanation that he boarded the 'Mother Plane' and is still alive, presumably to this day, given that he was the earthly embodiment of Allah.

The 'Plane' to which they refer is in the shape of a huge wheel built in Japan in 1929 and launched into outer space. The UFO sightings reported around the world are invariably sightings of this very craft. No, really.

Indeed, Minister Louis Farrakhan, the organisation's leader from 1975 to 2007, claimed he himself had seen the sacred craft, in a vision he had had in 1985. He claimed he was carried up to 'a wheel, or unidentified flying object, and heard the voice of Elijah Muhammad, the leader of NOI from 1934 to 1975.

And if you believe that, you'll probably also believe Elijah Muhammad's creation theory in *Message To The Black Man in America*. This states that white people are a race of devils created on a Greek island by a black scientist called Yakub who arranged for a plan of eugenics killing all but light-skinned babies over a 600-year period, until he had made a race of white people who could take over the world, conquering and enslaving the original man. Why on earth he would want to do this remains decidedly hazy, but either way, this new race was released abroad to spread disharmony among the original race and thereby come to rule the original man for thousands of years.

This theory may reflect the fact that eugenics was the fashionable subject of the day in scientific circles in the 1930s, a different form of which the Nazis would adopt with devastating consequences. Then again, in that instance, maybe the Jews were their own worst enemies. Farrakhan and friends seem to think so.

'Poor Jews died while big Jews were at the root of what you call the Holocaust,' he argued in 1995, while his assistant Khalid Muhammad said a couple of years earlier, 'everybody always talk about Hitler exterminating six million Jews... but don't nobody ever asked what did they do to Hitler? What did they do to them folks?'

'They went in there, in Germany,' he said, 'the way they do everywhere they go, and they supplanted, they usurped, they turned around, and a German, in his own country, would almost have to go to a Jew to get money. They had undermined the very fabric of the society.'

Despite suffering from ill health which forced him to step down from the leadership of NOI in 2007, Farrakhan is still coming up with some interesting ideas. For instance, he told a rally in 2009 that the H1N1 flu vaccine was to be avoided, since it was developed to drive down the world's population.

'The Earth can't take 6.5 billion people,' he said. 'We just can't feed that many. So what are you going to do?... develop a science that kills them and makes it look as though they died from some disease.'

In summary, then, we must take issue with Chuck D's assertion from 'Bring The Noise': 'Farrakhan's a prophet and I think you oughta listen to what he can say to you.'

But on the other hand, Flavor Flav probably makes more sense.

Transcendental Meditation

Eastern religions and rock'n'roll were considered as closely related as broccoli and waterskiing before The Beatles took an interest in the late 1960s, but after George Harrison (Patient Zero in the spread of Eastern spiritualism in rock), recommended they all visit Maharishi Mahesh Yogi in India, there was no turning back.

However, the actual content of the Maharishi's teachings were rather more vague than you would expect for a religious sage. His sermons were summed up by *Time* magazine as 'How to succeed spiritually without really trying.'

Fellow Indian religious scholars condemned the Maharishi for promoting a programme of spiritual peace without either penance or asceticism. Which doesn't make him wrong, of course, but does make you wonder if a big part of his appeal to decadent Western rock stars was that he omitted any mention of having to lead a strict religious lifestyle or give up any material possessions. A rich man really could enter the kingdom of heaven.

Indeed, there were other parts of his philosophy which might also have reassured his more privileged followers that their riches were nothing more than their just desserts, in stark contrast to the scumbag classes they left behind.

'Everyone is his own responsibility,' he told Era Bell, editor of *Ebony*, in 1968. 'I cannot blame someone if I am poor. If I'm energetic and if I have imagination and clear thinking, I become wealthy.'

'Survival of the fittest is the law,' he added. Wow, the Maharishi and Mrs Thatcher – fellow travellers if they could only come together!

Furthermore, the war in Vietnam was not the fault of politicians, but 'frustrated, tense and worried' civilians. Still, if it floats your boat, where's the harm, huh? Trouble is, the numerous scientific studies into its benefits suggest… there aren't any. The Agency for Healthcare Research and Quality was one of many who couldn't find any evidence to recommend it, concluding in 2007: 'TM® had no advantage over health education to improve measures of systolic blood pressure and diastolic blood pressure, body weight, heart rate, stress, anger, self-efficacy, cholesterol, dietary intake, and level of physical activity in hypertensive patients.'

Still, the Maharishi's no longer around to defend himself, and we mustn't speak ill of the dead. We wouldn't want to come back as a pauper.

Satanism

OK, do we have any Satanists in the house?

Hello? Hello?!

It's OK, you can admit it, you're among friends, and no one's judging here.

Silence

Right, so no one, out of all the millions… well, thousands… ok, dozens of readers of this book, is actually a Satanist?

Come on! This is rock'n'roll! The devil's music! Surely, by law of averages there must be someone who's not just playing around when they sing along to 'Highway To Hell' or 'Sympathy For The Devil'? No?

Incredible. After 80-odd years of beckoning forth Satan's diabolical spirit, it turns out that everyone has been taking all this devil-flirting about as seriously as an Alice Cooper on-stage execution.

Even rock's most militant Beelzebub-botherers will invariably back down from horn-fondling when pressed to explain their views in detail.

Deicide's Glenn Benton, for instance, who branded an upside down cross on his forehead, and Varg 'Count Grisnackh' Vikernes, who murdered his bandmate and helped burn down numerous churches, both now disown the Satanist label.

Maybe the problem is that Satanism is such a broad, erm, church. There are two loosely defined wings of Satanism and they are as follows:

1. Atheistic Satanism

This is the kind where followers do not actually believe in any deity, but use Satan as a symbol of opposition to organised religion. So, erm, they're Satanists who don't really believe in Satan.

2. Theistic Satanism

This kind incorporates a myriad of views, whose common link is a reverence for Satan chiefly for his supposed commitment to hedonism and selfish indulgence. To quote one broad summary of Satanist beliefs:

'Satan represents indulgence instead of abstinence; Satan represents vengeance instead of turning the other cheek; and Satan represents all of the so-called sins, as they all lead to physical, mental, or emotional gratification.'

If all the various strands of Satanism have one thing in common, though, it's a firm commitment to being uncommitted to anything except their own selfish ends, and screw the rest of us. And therein lies its fatal flaw as a religion: Why would you want to worship any higher power if the power of your own free will is all that really matters?

Both Glenn Benton and the avowed Norwegian Theistic Satanist and metal-merchant Jon Nodtveidt advocated suicide, claiming 'death is the ultimate orgasm'. The latter even went ahead and killed himself. Admirable commitment, perhaps, but I have a feeling that promoting suicide among your followers might have a negative impact on numbers at the next Luciferian Order coffee morning.

So, you can't help concluding that all forms of Satanism are, at heart, little more than childish contrarianism based entirely around ignoring all other social hindrances to free will and, more importantly, upsetting those who try to impose them. In which case, congratulations, Satanists everywhere You have succeeded in annoying everyone. Now kindly stop wasting our time.

SOME MIGhT SAy
STICKS AND ROLLING STONES

'His kind of music is deplorable, a rancid smelling aphrodisiac. It fosters almost totally negative and destructive reactions in young people.'

Frank Sinatra on Elvis Presley, 1957

'There have been many accolades uttered about Elvis' talent and performances through the years, all of which I agree with wholeheartedly. I shall miss him dearly as a friend. He was a warm, considerate and generous man.'

Frank Sinatra on the late Elvis Presley, 1977

'He will see who'll sell the most records when this trial is over and it won't be him.'

Sid Vicious on Johnny Rotten, 1979

He was dead within weeks.

'He was such a lovely guy. You could see it in his eyes… when he was beating you up and he'd just stop and go, "I don't really want to do this."'

Malcolm Owen of The Ruts on Sid Vicious, 1979

Marilyn, 'You Don't Love Me'
Jaz: This is dreadful, right? He's got an awful voice but I suppose it'll appeal to little girls and faggots… between you me and the gas chamber, I think… well, I'll leave it to your imagination what should be done to people like this…

Jaz Coleman from Killing Joke reviews the singles, 1984

… and the introduction to this feature admits: 'Some of what they said we couldn't/wouldn't print'!

'It's hard to beat Led Zeppelin's creativity, but… they weren't as exciting as Def Leppard.'

Herman Rarebell, Scorpions, 1984

'Robbie Williams and the Spice Girls, all they basically are is f**king children's TV presenters.'

Blur's Alex James, 1999

Alex James was last heard of as The Sun's *food writer – an infinitely more noble vocation, I'm sure you'll agree.*

'All that money, and he's still got hair like a fucking dinner lady.'

Boy George on Elton John, 2010

'That Black Eyed Peas "Dirty Dancing" thing is worse than raping a cat. What is wrong with people? Do they hate ears?'.

LCD Soundsystem's James Murphy, via Twitter, 2011

Popular music was once the domain of simple pleasures. But ever since The Beatles grew their first beards, musicians have felt qualified to touch on weighty academic topics within their lyrics. The only problem is, sometimes they don't actually know what they're singing about. Now settle down, children, face the front and let the lesson begin...

BACK TO SchOOL 9.

WEIGHTY SUBJECTS THAT POPULAR SONGS HAVE TACKLED... BADLY

hiSTORy

'Early morning, April 4, Shot rings out, in the Memphis Sky,
Free at last, they took your life, They could not take your pride.'

U2, 'Pride (In The Name Of Love)'

Thank you, Hewson, for your rather touching composition about the late US civil rights leader Martin Luther King. I'm sorry? No, I won't call you 'Bono', while you're in my class you'll be Paul Hewson. And take off those shades, boy, we've been sat indoors for the last half an hour.

Now, I appreciate your empathy for Dr King who, as those of you who have been paying attention will know, was shot dead by an assassin's bullet on 4 April 1968. But while a shot may well have rung out in the Memphis sky that morning, it wouldn't have been the one that took his life. Why? Because that one was fired at 6.01pm. I guess 'Just after teatime, April 4?' wouldn't have scanned quite so well, eh, Hewson?

'My, my, at Waterloo, Napoleon did surrender.'

ABBA, 'Waterloo'

Except he didn't, did he? If only these cocky Scandinavian scoundrels had stopped a moment to consult their history books properly, they would discover that Napoleon did *not* surrender but only retreated from Waterloo (in Belgium, not a train station in South London) into Rochefort, and it was there that he finally surrendered *four weeks later*.

You might think this nothing more than a hippy's split hair in the wider scheme of things. But in any just world, surely this glaring fault in their lyrics should have meant them being docked crucial points at the Eurovision Song Contest in 1974, in which this song triumphed. Imagine the repercussions if it had cost them victory! Bjorn Ulvaeus, their chief lyricist, would have resigned from pop music in shame, ABBA would have split after being pelted with rotten fruit at Stockholm airport, and a glittering career might never have got off the ground.

It is on tiny matters like these that empires can stand or fall. Now, Ulvaeus, you might like to look at Boney M's 'Rasputin', for an example of how to do historical pop with a bit of *real* gravitas...

> 'In a time where dinosaurs walked the earth, when the land was swamp and caves were home... to search for landscapes men would roam.'

Iron Maiden, 'Quest For Fire'

OK, so we'll go over it one more time just for you chaps over there with the studded wristbands.

First, there were the dinosaurs.

Then they died out, possibly due to climate change, possibly due to a comet, but that's not important right now. Anyway, approximately *65 MILLION YEARS* later, *homo-sapiens* got up on his hind legs, and eventually, evolved into what we now know as 'Man'. But AT NO POINT WHATSOEVER IN HISTORY DID MEN SHARE THE EARTH WITH DINOSAURS. NEVER. NOT EVEN FOR A FEW MINUTES. IT DIDN'T HAPPEN. IS THAT CLEAR?!

Bob Dylan,'John Wesley Harding'

'John Wesley Harding was a friend to the poor,' claimed the voice of a generation back in 1968. 'He travelled with a gun in every hand... but he was never known to hurt an honest man.'

Dylan based the title track of his album on wild West outlaw and gunfighter John Wesley Hardin. The fact that he didn't bother looking up the correct spelling of his hero's name perhaps reflects a reluctance to overburden himself with research, so I feel duty bound to qualify his claims for the benefit of listeners who might have laboured under the impression that this was a reliable account of Hardin(g)'s life.

Hardin claimed to have killed 42 men, most of them Union soldiers or law enforcement officers trying to either capture him or prevent his escape. His last murder was said to have been the random shooting of a Mexican stranger for a $5 bet. Now, I don't know any of his victims personally, but law of averages suggests at least one of them might just have been an 'honest man' or, at the very least, not entirely deserving of dying at the hands of a gun-happy outlaw, as Dylan seems to suggest. An even stronger possibility is that John Wesley Hardin wasn't quite the noble rebel our Bob is at pains to portray him as. Still, nice tune.

MATHEMATICS

'Y'all niggas is scared, I'm your worst nightmare squared. That's double for niggas who ain't mathematically aware.'

Common, 'Making A Name For Ourselves (Featuring Canibus)'

Pull those trousers up and stop fidgeting, Mr Common, and pay attention, please. I appreciate your attempts to 'educate' your 'niggas', but I think perhaps you should have listened a little more carefully in class.

If you squared yourself, you would be left with… yourself. 'Squared' does not mean double, it means 'multiplied by itself'. If you squared the pair of you, you would indeed be doubled, so perhaps you might like to revise that line to say *we're* your worst nightmare squared. And don't tell tales on Mr Canibus and say it was his fault, Common. He might have delivered that line, but it's your name on the top of the lyric sheet.

BIOLOGY

'Now I guess I gotta tell 'em/That I got no cerebellum.'

The Ramones, 'Teenage Lobotomy'

Those of you who invariably look to cartoon punk bands for education in scientific matters will be dismayed to learn that Johnny, Joey and the other ones cannot be trusted when it comes to brain surgery issues. The removal of the cerebellum would do much more than cure mental illness, as a frontal lobotomy was once believed to do. Since the cerebellum is responsible for motor skills, the removal of the cerebellum would leave you a virtual vegetable. Is that what you want, Mr Ramone? Well is it?

'This morning at 4.50, I took her rather nifty. Down to an incubator where thirty minutes later. She gave birth to a daughter, within a year a walker.'

Squeeze, 'Up The Junction'

I have it on sound medical authority that no woman has ever given birth in an incubator. Even if she was distinctly tiny, and very, very ill.

RELIGIOUS EDUCATION

'As God has shown us, by turning stones to bread... '

USA for Africa, 'We Are the World'

It's so disappointing when musicians display ignorance of the gospels. God probably could turn stones to bread if he felt like opening his own artisan bakery, as he could probably do most things. But there is no mention of him doing any such thing in the Bible. Jesus came close, and as our Lord's earthly representative, we could probably let it pass if he had gone ahead and performed this miraculous feat. But Jesus did not actually do it either. According to Matthew 4:3, he was tempted by the devil to try turning stones to bread after fasting for forty days and nights in the wilderness, but he realised it was a test, and he stayed strong.

'Man cannot live by bread alone,' he concluded in Matthew 4:1–4 'but by every word that proceeds out of the mouth of God.'

Chew on that, do-gooders.

'A spaceman came traveling on his ship from afar/'twas light years of time since his mission did start.'

Chris De Burgh, 'A Spaceman Came Travelling'

I don't mean to piss on your Christmas log fire, Chris, but a light year is a unit not of time, but of distance. Stick to singing gloopy ballads to gullible birds in dresses.

'Your poses turn the passive into maniacs.'

The Beautiful South, '36D'

The debate about the effect of pornography still rages fiercely in certain circles, but after decades of research, no one has produced convincing evidence that looking at pictures of a young lady's breasts in a national newspaper warps men's minds to the point where they turn into rapists and murderers. Yet Paul Heaton has no hesitation in blaming eye-candy soft porn for rape in this lyrical assault on Page Three girls from 1992.

He also opines that 'You've turned our young men into dribbling clowns.' Strikingly similar, in both cases, to Islamic fundamentalists' argument for women wearing burqas, lest their exposed flesh inflame the unholy passions of previously moral menfolk and turn them into drooling, out-of-control monsters. The brazen temptresses!

It also sneers at the glamour models who choose to conduct themselves in this way and concludes 'You cheapen and you nasty every woman in this land'. Strong words. What woman, whatever land they happen to be in, would want to be 'nastied' by anyone, male or female?

And there we are, thinking that the goal of feminism was not to restrict women's lifestyle or career choices, but to emancipate them, so that they can pursue the career of their choice and present themselves as they see fit, without fear of being burned at the stake for displaying their bodies, or condemned as 'traitors' to their own sex, in much the same way as they were back in less enlightened times when they failed to conform to society's codes of conduct. Maybe the title 'Get thee to a Nunnery' would have been more apposite.

GEOGRAPHY

'Sometimes the sun goes round the moon.'

Vanessa Williams, 'Saved The Best For Last'

See me after school, Miss Williams, please.

'Thunder only happens when it's raining.'

Fleetwood Mac, 'Dreams'

Must try harder, Mr Mac.

'How can we dance when our earth is turning?'

Midnight Oil, 'Beds Are Burning'

Now, let me introduce you to the concept of gravity...

'New York to East California, there's a new wave coming, I warn ya.'

The residents of the west of California, where most of the population of that state lives, would have been relieved and offended in equal measure not to be included in this 'new wave'. Would they have missed out on a highly acclaimed punk-pop movement of the late 1970s and early 1980s? Or stayed dry during an absolutely enormous, continent-engulfing tsunami?

'Coast to coast, LA to Chicago... '

Sade, 'Smooth Operator '

Now, Miss Adu, if I can just show you this basic, easy-to-understand map of the USA, we have LA, over here on one coast, and then here we have Chicago... sort of towards the top, but in the middle, and nowhere near the coast. Shall we have another go at that one, then?

CLASSICS

'Egyptians developed all sciences of the mind/To the point where they ruled the planet.'

Boogie Down Productions, 'You Must Learn' (remix)

This neat summary of prehistory from KRS One is derived directly from a philosophy known as Afrocentrism. Its central claim is that African Americans should trace their roots back to Ancient Egypt because it was dominated by a race of black Africans.

Being in the pay of the white, judaeo-christian establishment, it is sadly inevitable that I would doubt that claim, but anyway, here's what The Man told me to say:

KRS One's claim that Egyptians pioneered 'sciences of the mind' is promoted in George James' 1954 book *Stolen Legacy*, which in turn was heavily influenced by the teachings of black nationalist Marcus Garvey, who believed that in order to redress the balance of power between the races black children should be taught that they are superior.

American Classics Professor Mary Lefkowitz makes several salient points in her book *Not Out of Africa: How Afrocentrism Became an Excuse to Teach Myth As History.* She points out that many of James' theories come from sources predating the understanding of Egyptian hieroglyphics, and notes that James' claim that Aristotle stole his ideas from the great library at Alexandria fails to consider the rather obstructive fact that the library wasn't founded until after his death.

Professor Clarence E. Walker of the University of California, who is African American, called Afrocentrism 'racist, reactionary, and essentially therapeutic. It suggests that nothing important has happened in black history since the time of the pharaohs and thus trivializes the history of Black Americans. Afrocentrism places an emphasis on Egypt that is, to put it bluntly, absurd.'

However, his rhymes were rubbish, unlike KRS One's, and his beats and samples totally wack, unlike BDP's, which may be part of the reason why Afrocentrism continues to enjoy a highly-respected position in hip-hop culture.

Bob Dylan, 'Hurricane'

Here we are presented with an impassioned argument for the alleged wrongful conviction of boxer Rubin Carter, on the stirring opening track from his 1976 album *Desire*.

However, the counsel for the defence doesn't do his case a huge amount of good when he describes Carter as 'The number one contender for the middleweight crown.' Carter was in fact only the ninth-ranked contender at the time of the murder, and at no point was he a number one contender.

Mr Dylan then points out weaknesses in the prosecution case by indicating that the police's use of a dying victim as a witness was problematic due to his failing eyesight. 'Although this man could hardly see,' he sings, 'They told him that he could identify the guilty man.'

Thus the witness's testimony is, with some justification, considered unreliable by the learned Mr. Dylan. However, later in the same song, Dylan reports: 'Four in the morning and they haul Rubin (the defendant) in… The wounded man looks up through his one dying eye, says, "What'd you bring him in here for? He ain't the guy!"'

So, Mr Dylan, was he a reliable witness or not? Either his poor eyesight makes any testimony invalid, or it backs up both contradictory statements.

I put it to you, Mr, Dylan, that you actually have NO IDEA what went on that night, and therefore cannot be considered a reliable narrator of this song.

Just as well Bob wasn't called to the stand, then.

INTERNATIONAL STUDIES

Manic Street Preachers, 'Yes'

'In these plagued streets of pity you can buy anything… ' sang the Manics in this startlingly bleak picture of unspeakable exploitation in an unnamed locale. 'He's a boy,' they continue, 'You want a girl so cut off his cock. Tie his hair in bunches, fuck him, call him Rita if you want.'

The Manics made their name on the back of an unflinching willingness to rub humanity's nose in its own steaming waste. But on this occasion I suspect lyricist Richey Edwards, might have been taking artistic licence a bit further than the perimeters of proven fact.

Where exactly were these plagued streets of pity? I mean, I know South Wales had endured some lean times during Richey's formative years, but news of DIY sex changes combined with rape, genital mutilation and enforced hairdressing somehow escaped the gaze of either the media, the law or Amnesty International during the years preceding the song's release in 1994.

Perhaps he's talking about foreign climes – after all, the song begins and ends with samples from the 1993 documentary film *Hookers, Hustlers, Pimps, and their Johns*. But I would imagine that wherever in the world it occurred, even someone with specialist knowledge of sex change operations would struggle to remove their son's penis and rape him without their victim dying from blood loss in the process, which might be a little self-defeating.

In summary then: I'VE TOLD YOU A MILLION TIMES, EDWARDS – DON'T EXAGGERATE!

SOME MIGHT SAY

WHY MUSIC AND CLAIRVOYANCE DON'T MIX.

'It will be gone by June.'

Variety magazine on rock'n'roll, March 1955

'Stick to driving a truck, because you're never going to make it as a singer.'

Band leader Eddie Bond to Elvis Presley after the latter auditioned as a singer in 1954

After Elvis had his first hit single, Bond contacted him and asked if he wanted to join his band after all. Elvis politely declined the invitation.

'We don't like their sound, and guitar music is on the way out.'

Decca records A&R department on The Beatles, 1962

A&R chief Dick Rowe was said to have been responsible for passing on them. He didn't make that mistake again though. Soon after he signed an unknown bunch of blues scruffs called The Rolling Stones.

'The singer will have to go. The BBC won't like him.'

The Rolling Stones' first manager, Eric Easton, to his business partner, when first seeing the band in action, 1963

'A guitar's alright John… but you'll never earn a living by it.'

John Lennon's Aunt Mimi, to the teenage John who had lived with her since childhood, 1950s

In 1965, John bought a bungalow for her in Poole in Dorset. For her new home, he gave her a stone tablet inscribed with the above quote.

'Well obviously we can't keep playing the same sort of music until we're 40, because when we're old men playing "From Me To You", nobody's going to want to know about that sort of thing'.

Paul McCartney, 1964

'I think they [The Beatles] will maintain strong teenage appeal for two or three years. After that, maybe they will become really established film stars.

Brian Epstein, 1965

'I'd rather be dead than singing "Satisfaction" when I'm 45.'

Mick Jagger, 1969

What's the betting he'll still be singing it when he's 85?

'I once told a journalist that if I could go back in time I'd find Adolf Hitler and stop him. It came out that I'd like to meet Hitler.'

Thus spake Clark Datchler of Johnny Hates Jazz in the twilight of his prime and his complaint is a familiar one to anyone residing within the peripheral vision of the public eye.

A casual aside can be turned into an inflammatory statement, a spoof quote becomes a regular on celebrities-are-stupid internet lists and you would never convince people that the words never emitted from your mouth even if you took out a half-hour television advert before the evening news in every English speaking nation on Earth.

Who knows, among the many quotes included in this book, there may be several which were misheard, misinterpreted or – the old classic – 'taken out of context'. If so, I am truly sorry. Or at least, mildly contrite. But by way of doing our bit to right wrongs, we can confirm that the following commonly attributed sayings in this chapter did NOT come from the individuals often associated with them...

Myth-Quoted

10.

FAMOUS THINGS ARTISTS (PROBABLY) NEVER SAID

'The only thing negroes can do for me is shine my shoes and buy my records'

Elvis Presley, 1950s

This rogue gob-morsel began spreading as far back as April 1957, and passed into 'fact', not helped by a mention in Albert Goldman's dirt-digging biography *Elvis*.

Yet The King was never directly quoted saying any such thing, he always denied it vehemently, and those close to him have attested to his total lack of racial prejudice.

Michael T. Bertrand, writing in *Race, Rock and Elvis*, pins down the origin of this quote to an April 1957 article where an anonymous 'person on the street' offered it as their opinion as to what Elvis might have thought of his black audience. It since passed into folklore as a direct quote from the man himself.

Such mitigation didn't stop Public Enemy from giving him both barrels on their 1989 polemic 'Fight The Power'.

'Elvis was a hero to most,' boomed Chuck D, 'But he never meant shit to me you see, Straight up racist that sucker was, simple and plain… '

In contrast, a quote in *The Washington Post* around the time of that single's release, from Public Enemy's Professor Griff, informed us: 'Jews are responsible for the majority of the wickedness in the world'. We're still waiting to find out which 'context' that one was taken out of besides his own stupid mouth.

'If I could find a white boy who could sing like a nigger, I could make a million dollars'

Sam Phillips, Owner of Elvis Presley's label Sun records, circa 1954

Immediately we are forced to scotch another dubious claim of racism aimed at white Southerners, as another Albert Goldman claim in *Elvis* was cast into major doubt by Sun records co-manager Marion Keisker, who is on tape insisting Phillips did not use the offensive 'N' word but in fact said 'If I could find a white man with the negro sound, and the negro feel, I could make a billion dollars'. A much less offensive statement. However, Phillips himself denied ever saying either of those things. Make up your own mind, but for this onlooker, this quote would fit just a little too neatly into the theory that the whole Elvis phenomenon was part of a neat masterplan by a cynical, racist southern huckster. The world of music, as we will learn elsewhere in this pages, is rarely, if ever, that well-planned.

'Before Elvis, there was nothing'

John Lennon, 1965

This, it turns out, was a rather presumptuous paraphrasing from a quote Lennon gave in 1965 after meeting Elvis. He admitted that if there'd been no Elvis there would have been no Beatles, but his claim that there was 'nothing' before the King was also allegedly said to have been said of Cliff and the Shadows, before whose emergence in the UK there was also 'nothing'. Conclusions from which are fairly thin on the ground, apart from the fact that things really must have been pretty bloody grim back then.

'Nul points' (pronounced 'nul pwah')

Eurovision song contest judges, 1970s and ever since, allegedly

Whenever that time of year comes around again, as sure as a camera follows Kim Kardashian, all newspapers will refer light-heartedly to acts who registered 'nul points' (pronounced 'null pwah') in previous years' contests.

The phrase refers to the total repeatedly announced by those hilarious foreign types when reading out the scores in several languages. For instance 'Norway – no points – nul points – keine Pünkte.'

It's the gag that keeps on giving. The only problem being: no-one said it in the first place.

As any regular viewer of Europe's favourite musical extravaganza can confirm, the only scores that are announced are those of the acts who have been awarded between one and 12 points.

And even if it had been announced, it wouldn't be described as 'nul points' or even the grammatically accurate 'nul point'. They would say 'pas de point' or 'zero point'.

Be sure to regale your friends with that one at your next 'Eurovision party'.

'Writing about music is like dancing about architecture'

Elvis Costello, 1980s

Supposedly the ultimate put-down to music journalists, numerous non-fool-suffering musicians have been cited as the person behind this maxim, but Costello and numerous others including Frank Zappa have both denied originating the quote, even though Costello did say in *Musician* magazine in 1983: 'Writing about music is like dancing about architecture—it's a really stupid thing to want to do.' According to the sterling investigative work from www.quoteinvestigator.com, a similar saying has been doing the rounds since shortly after the First World War, when *New Republic* wrote: writing about music is as illogical as singing about economics.

The more recent version of the saying appears to have come from American comedy actor, satirist and painter Martin Mull in the late 1970s, when he said: 'Writing about painting is like dancing about architecture.'

Costello also credits Martin Mull for the saying. So hats off to him. And now I've got the chance to reply, Martin, I should point out that talking about writing about painting is like trampolining about knitting about botany. Stitch that, smart arse.

'AIDS is God's way of punishing gays'

Donna Summer, 1985

In 1983, disco queen Donna Summer was quoted as telling a fan after a show in Atlantic City, New Jersey, something along the lines of the above statement.

The story spread rapidly throughout the homosexual community, and her gay icon status was unofficially rescinded until further notice.

The story goes that a man with AIDS asked her to pray for him, and as a born again Christian, Summer said she would be delighted. She was heckled and accused of hypocrisy due to her recent conversion to born-again Christianity, and in the ensuing discussion, Summer was said to have voiced her opinion that AIDS appeared in the gay community because of people's 'reckless lifestyles'.

Controversial and misguided perhaps, but not exactly the same as what her words were turned into a few Chinese whispers later. She duly prayed with the fan and embraced him, but the 'God's punishment' rumour soon became bigger than the fact.

Since then, she has since stated on numerous occasions that she never said anything of the sort.

As early as 1985, she issued a statement saying, 'It's very difficult for me to believe that this terrible misunderstanding continues. Since the very beginning of my career I have had tremendous support and friendship from... the gay community. It is a source of great concern to me that anything I may have said has cast me as homophobic.'

In 1989, she spelt it out even more clearly in a letter to Act-Up, the Aids activist group. 'I did not say God is punishing gays with AIDS,' she says, 'I did not sit with ill intentions in judgment over your lives. I haven't stopped talking to my friends who are gay, nor have I ever chosen my friends by their sexual preferences.'

Since she has continued to work with AIDS charities ever since, so I guess actions speak louder than words, whatever they may have been.

'Give us your fucking money'

Bob Geldof on Live Aid, 1985

It is the moment everyone seems to remember from the BBC's coverage of the 12-hour Live Aid charity gig at Wembley. Frustrated with the fact that viewers were evidently having a jolly good time but forgetting the point of the whole exercise, a tired and, inevitably, emotional Geldof visibly lost patience with the presenters and resorted to industrial language to get his point across.

That much is true, but over the years that followed, his exact words somehow got completely changed to be simplified into a simple and heartfelt order of 'Give us your fucking money.'

In fact he wasn't quite that blunt. Instead, flanked by the never-to-be-repeated gathering of The Cult's Ian Astbury, Billy Connolly and Pamela Stephenson, he prodded a finger sharply into the table in front of him and barked: 'There are people dying NOW.'

As he went on to ask for the phone number for credit card donations, presenter David Hepworth got a message in his ear from behind the scenes, and explained that first they would be showing the address to send money in.

'Fuck the address,' snapped Geldof, 'let's get the numbers, because that's how we're going to get it.'

Much embarrassed but amused shuffling followed before Hepworth sheepishly admitted: 'I think we're going to have to have the address first.'

The address was indeed shown, followed by the phone lines, but the power of the four-letter word had already been unleashed. The viewing public got the message, and the money began to pour in. Cocking good effort, Bob.

'Ringo isn't even the best drummer in the Beatles'

John Lennon, 1968

This is said to have been the late Beatle's typically acerbic reply when asked if Ringo was the best drummer in the world. It is a reference to fellow Fab Paul McCartney's considerable ability behind the kit. Yet for all the forensic chronicling of the Fab Four's every thought, word and deed during their lifespan as a band, no one seems to be able to reliably identify a time, place or context in which John ever said those words.

Some assume it was one of the throwaway quips offered during those early American interviews around 1964–65, and even cite Ringo as originating it as a self-deprecating one-liner. Others point to the period where Ringo briefly took his drumsticks home in August 1968 and his bandmates responded with a show of love and respect for his uniquely uncomplicated rhythmic chops.

An appraisal of Ringo as 'Probably the best drummer in the world right now' was actually made by George Martin in 1968, and you would have thought that the quote might have come in response to an interviewer asking Lennon to endorse this view, but no such soundbite seems to have been forthcoming.

Wikipedia cites their own reference for this quote as 'Manning (2008)'… but there doesn't appear to have been anything ever published about The Beatles by anyone named Manning apart from a gag by a certain Mr. B. Manning of The Embassy Club, Manchester. It's at this point that the tell-tale signs of apocrypha seem too numerous to ignore.

Even if he did say it, it certainly wouldn't appear to be a case of many a true word spoken in jest. Lennon's enduring regard for Ringo is demonstrated by the fact he hired him to perform on his first solo album and as late as September 1980, he could be found paying tribute in a *Playboy* interview thus: 'Whatever that spark is in Ringo that we all know but can't put our finger on... there is something in him that is projectable and he would have surfaced with or without The Beatles. Ringo is a damn good drummer.'

So I think we can safely accept that Lennon's words did not reflect his true opinions on the matter. Whether he said it at all is also open to considerable doubt. Unless, of course, there are any Beatles anoraks out there who can prove otherwise...

'When I watch TV and see those poor starving kids all over the world, I can't help but cry. I mean I'd love to be skinny like that, but not with all those flies and death and stuff'

Mariah Carey, 1990s

Many things that pop stars say are described as 'beyond parody'. This quote from 1996 would have fitted squarely into that category... if only it hadn't been a parody, from a satirical website called *Cupcake*. It was subsequently quoted in *Vox*, the music magazine, and then *The Independent*. And henceforth, the farthest reaches of the World Wide Web.

'I'm inconsolable... He was the greatest basketball player the world has ever seen'

Mariah Carey on the death of the King of Jordan, 1990s

Arf! These pop stars aren't half dim, aren't they? Except not quite this dim. This pearler was made up on an internet posting to a fansite in 1999, and later falsely attributed to both *CNN* and *USA Today*.

'I'd rather have my children starve than have
white people buy one of my albums'

Lauryn Hill, 1990s

The story spread that the newly solo Fugees singer Lauryn Hill had said
the above, or similar sentiments, in an MTV interview. That claim was
first made by a caller to Howard Stern's radio show, and soon became
common currency, to the point that Eminem even referred to it in his
1999 track 'Cum On Everybody', quipping 'Bought Lauryn Hill's tape so
her kids could starve.'

However, no recording of this alleged quote has ever surfaced –
a little strange considering it was supposedly uttered before the cameras
of a global TV network,

'I get to go to lots of overseas places...
like Canada'

Britney Spears, *Blender*, 2004

It's rare that these quotes have a source sited, but Britney Spears is
supposed to have said this in an April 2004 issue of *Blender*. Imagine
our surprise, then, to find she was not featured at all in the April 2004
issue of Blender. She was featured in January of that year, but that
quote is strangely absent from the piece. And no other source can be
found for it anywhere. That hasn't stopped the entire internet and their
next-door neighbours repeating it as one of the dumbest ever celebrity
quotes including such respected outlets as imdb.com and, erm, *The Sun*.
And on the very same lists, you'll find this one...

'I've never really wanted to go to Japan. Simply
because I don't like eating fish. And I know
that's very popular out there in Africa'

Britney Spears, 2000s

This one has a touch of a rubbish stand-up comedian about it, but it's
still quoted regularly. The fact that when you Google 'fish japan britney'
you can also find footage of Britney eating sushi in Japan around the

same time, and also see various other mentions of her listing sushi as one of her favourite foods suggests this is deep fried baloney, invented to make that familiar, razor-sharp satirical point – female pop stars are not very bright.

'So, where's the Cannes Film Festival being held this year?'

Christina Aguilera, 2007

Once again, the tell-tale lack of attribution when this is mentioned will throw up a fishy smell to any connoisseur of urban myths. The US diva, we are often told, 'famously' said this. But it wasn't quoted anywhere at the time, and although it first began appearing in 2007, there were no reports of her saying it before the festival began. So unless you know different, I'm lumping that in with the Britney quotes as more popstrel-baiting bollocks. And can it be mere coincidence that all these are alleged to come from young women?

'It's important to be thankful, even if you're poor. I mean, come on, we all have clean water – well OK, not people in the developing world'

Avril Lavigne, Q, October 2007

The then 22-year-old Canadian has vehemently denied making the statements attributed to her in a Q magazine 'Ten Commandments' feature. Speaking to a Canadian radio station, she said, 'Q Magazine had all these false quotes that I didn't put and the press over here made a big deal about it.' Whether 'false' means 'very slightly tweaked to make some kind of sense' (the piece was presented as a series of long quotes) or 'completely invented' is not entirely clear. Suffice it to say, as one of Q's most long-serving, highly-respected and sexually attractive contributors, I can confirm that they would never knowingly employ dishonest writers.

The discerning pop picker has never had more opportunities to read about his or her favourite art form than they do these days. Newspapers, magazines and now websites and blogs deluge music lovers with carefully crafted words to help enhance enjoyment of this most mercurial of art forms.

However, music critics do have a distinct tendency to overuse certain words. And they can't always be taken at face value. So, from a man who has used at least three-quarters of these terms, here's an indispensable guide to some phrases you're guaranteed to encounter, and the fascinating subtext behind them...

A REAL RETURN to FORM

11.

SOME VERY OVERUSED WORDS IN POPULAR MUSIC WRITING

ON the COVER

A selection of spurious boasts, empty promises and questionable claims found on magazine covers and website home pages... and what they really mean.

Voted magazine of the year - again!
Voted magazine of the year – by our publisher.

His most revealing interview ever!
... apart from the one he had at the exotic sexual disease clinic last Monday afternoon.

Her most revealing interview ever!
Lady Gaga's talking about her quincy again.

Your questions answered
Our questions answered. We make them up in the office because yours are always 'when are you next going to play in Malaysia?'

Sex, Drugs, Rock 'n' Roll... and me
Sex is a very private thing for me, I've recently stopped taking drugs (like I said I had the last four times you interviewed me), my new album's the best I've ever made... Can I go now?'

'This might be our last album'
'... until the next one'.

The 50 best...
The 50 best options we had for the cover all fell through.

... as you've never seen them before
We persuaded them to put on some hats.

That spat with XXXXXXX - What really happened
Answer – nothing.

Exclusive interview
No-one else was actually in the room with us on this occasion, but the 114 other media representatives queuing up outside the hotel room may also have interviewed this person for their respective publications. Still, ours is better.

On the road with...
Ten minutes on the steps of the tour bus with…

An intimate portrait
They gave us two minutes in a corridor to do the shots, so the photographer tried in vain to make it look interesting by getting right in their grill and shooting black and white. What do you want, blood?

Intimate shots
The photographer told them to just 'act as if I'm not there', while shoving a camera lens up their right nostril.

...bares all
… no, you don't get to see her bottom, she just talks a bit about 'media intrusion' and you see her naked shoulder in the pics.

In bed with...
We persuaded them to lie in a bed for some photos. We did not get in, let alone have sex with them.

What happened when... Lou Reed met the Strokes?

A lot of mumbling, some moaning, a bit of shuffling about, hours of waiting, precious little else.

The SEX issue

We don't care what kind of tragic pervert you are, please, please, please buy this magazine.

The 61 best new...

We've been desperate enough to pay a marketing consultant half our yearly editorial budget to tell us that odd numbers sometimes seem to help sell magazines.

The 113 best downloads/Youtube/Twitter/Facebook moments

Apparently no one buys music any more – will you buy our magazine if we mention the internet?

'The truth about me, Courtney, and the silk stockings.'

'The truth? I helped fix her fan belt. No, not in that way.'

More than 278 albums reviewed

A couple of classic reissues get five star reviews. No albums get one star. No albums get zero stars. 254 albums get three stars. Any the wiser?

In the studio with...

Well, what else is there to do with Bloc Party?

Behind the scenes

That boring soundcheck in full boring glory.

Vote! Vote! Vote! For your _____ Awards winners

Vote! Vote! Vote! Preferably to a premium rate phone line, and then we might take your votes into account for one or two of the awards, but decide all the others by guaranteeing at least one award to each of the biggest names we can persuade to turn up at them. That way we might have a chance of getting the magazine logo on page 19 of the *Daily Mirror*.

The Untold Story

Are there any stories not yet told about The Beatles / Stones / Beach Boys in the sixties? This former Abbey Road teaboy reckons so…

'I almost died'

But as usual, I didn't. Instead, the doctor suggested I might consider refraining from smoking /drinking/injecting heroin into my toe.

100/1000/5645 albums/songs/artists you must hear before you die

Well, we say 'must', but we don't mean that in a punitive sense. You won't be dragged from your deathbed and the last vestiges of life beaten out of you by club-wielding taste police as penance for never having heard The Fall's *Live At The Witch Trials*. In fact, you may pass away blissfully in your sleep without the slightest lingering regret that despite a long, fulfilling and thrill-filled 107-year existence on planet earth, you never quite got around to checking out *Throbbing Gristle's DOA: The Third And Final Report*.

MAGAZINE REVIEWS

Some common adjectives, references and descriptions the discerning consumer may be confronted with…

'Dark'

During the golden age of pop, the idea of popular music being in any way 'dark' made about as much sense as children's S&M kits. But the gloomy textures and downbeat attitudes of alternative rock have now taken over the mainstream, just as sticky-up haircuts were once the domain of socially maladjusted heroin addicts who occasionally played bass for Nurse With Wound but are now to be found on the head of the sales manager in Currys.

So now you can't open a newspaper arts section without finding the word 'dark' used to describe anything from the new Batman movie to Delia's new recipe for spaghetti bolognese. Indeed, I understand that in interviews to promote their new nationwide tour, Pre-school pop favourites The Tweenies have been telling journalists how their new songs will be 'darker' and 'harder' in approach.

'Fiercely intelligent'

No, they won't devour your still twitching carcass while establishing the six trillionth place of pi – they're just quite bright.

'On acid'

No, not music that is for staring for six hours at a speck of paint on the wall wondering how the secrets of the Universe can be contained therein. Just some slightly weird music.

'Angular'

No, don't get your protractor out, it's just some jerky guitar music.

'That rare thing...'
No, not the Palos Verdes Blue butterfly, but a half-decent record.

'Landfill indie'
Popular, tuneful guitar pop that people actually buy and enjoy in their millions – eurgh! Get it away from me!

'Coldplay, Snow Patrol, Keane'
Bywords for 'bad' or 'bland'. Non-critics may also know it as 'Enjoyable, well-crafted, emotionally uplifting rock music with mass appeal'. Yuk!

'Sophomore effort'
I've read too many thunderously dull American music mags.

'It may not be _____ but if you're looking for _____ then you could do worse than this _____'
God this record is boring. But I've been told I've got to 'give them a fair hearing'. Bet you're already putting your shoes on and stampeding down to the record shop, right?

'-esque'
' –ish'. In French. And even in France they think it's a bit over used.

'A real return to form'
It's another mildly disappointing Bob Dylan/Rolling Stones/David Bowie/REM/Liam or Noel Gallagher album and we'd be delighted if they would kindly grace the cover of our magazine and give us an exclusive interview.

'His/their best since _____'
It's another mildly disappointing Bob Dylan/Rolling Stones/David Bowie/REM/Liam or Noel Gallagher album and we'd be delighted if they would kindly grace the cover of our magazine and give us an exclusive interview.

'Anthemic'
Lots of 'woah-ohs'.

'Widescreen production'
Too much reverb.

'Accessible'
Won't offend your grandparents.

'Should appeal to fans of...'
Does not appeal to me.

'_____ is worth the admission price alone'
But if the CD contained just the one song we're referring to you'd be sending the bloody thing to BBC Watchdog screaming blue murder.

'Sumptuous, sweeping'
No, not my Colombian cleaning lady, they've just chucked a string section on there.

'Epic'
You might want to make a brew while this one's on. Don't worry, it'll still be going when you get back.

'Über-'
'Over', or 'very', but suggesting, not entirely honestly, that the writer can understand German.

'Skittering drum'n'bass 'beats''
Radiohead are back again. Aren't you excited?

PREVIEWS

You may hear the following both from independent media outlets and the record company blurbs accompanying them. In both cases, beware: They speak with forked tongue…

'Mercury-nominated'
Worthy but dull.

'Edgy'
Anything with that distinctive cordite whiff of bloody revolution. You know, like, say, Pink. Or an *X Factor* contestant doing a Billy Idol song.

'Long-awaited new album'
Twice-rewritten new album, replete with cynically conceived, hastily-written 'hits' after the record company told them to go back and make something they could sell.

'Country-tinged'
The producer knows a pedal steel player.

'Dizzingly ambitious'
Ludicrously self-indulgent.

'Critically acclaimed'
Currently unclaimed in a pile in an independent label's warehouse.

'Guest appearance by Flea from the Chili Peppers'
Hollywood actor makes dreadful record.

 GENRES

Those unacquainted with the jargon and terminology associated with popular music will be ill-served by me going into the various genres and micro-genres in detail. So let's keep it simple:

`'Indie-pop'`
Pop for people who think pop is beneath them.

`'Indie-rock'`
Rock for people who think rock is beneath them.

`'Alt-rock'`
Rock for American people who think rock is beneath them.

`'Post-rock'`
Rock for people who think all of the above (and the below) is beneath them.

`'Intelligent techno'`
Dance music you can't dance to.

`'Ambient'`
Dance music you can't dance or listen to. Amazing light show, though…

`'Swamp blues'`
Twanging, quiffs, gravelly voices, mentions of the devil, Nick Cave's lawyers monitoring situation.

`'Americana'`
Neil Young-style whining, with added beards.

'Dub reggae'
Reggae with the good bits taken out.

'Cod reggae'
An often disparaged type of reggae with nice commercially-inclined pop tunes made by white people, as opposed to real authentic reggae, which is reggae with nice commercially-inclined pop tunes made by black people.

'_____-hop'
There's some sort of rapping going on at some point.

'_____tronica'
Are those bleeps? Possibly keyboards? Why yes, yes they are!

'Jungle'
Drum'n'bass, but only when made by scary black men in housing estates.

'Drum'n'bass'
Jungle, ever since it became racist to call it jungle or regard black men in housing estates as scary.

'UK garage'
Dance music made by poor kids in nightclubs between 1997 and 2004. Not to be confused with garage punk, made by poor kids in America between 1964 and 1970 and by rich kids in toilet venues ever since.

'Dubstep'
Garage you can't dance to.

'Grime'
A combination of the above three, with twice as many police harassing people outside the gigs.

A Real Return to Form **149**

fEATURES

'We caught up with...'

Reading this introductory line of many interviews, you'd imagine these meetings were performed during a morning jog, in which the journalist spotted the entire band out doing a few laps of the local park and managed to put on a sufficient burst of speed to accost them and talk about their new single. In fact, they are invariably pre-arranged through a manager and conducted in a hotel room or bar. Sorry for any confusion.

'Insert your own joke about _____'

I wouldn't be so crassly obvious as to make a joke about this subject, but if you could do my job for me, and insert your own joke about _____, that would be just tickety-boo.

'_____ imploded'

In music journalism, bands don't break up – they implode. As you can see, this sounds more revelatory than 'split up', because it suggests the band members have had some kind of violent reaction to each other (or one of them doesn't like the singer's girlfriend) but also demands that you paid attention in physics lessons at the age of 13 to know what it means. Besides, if they exploded they would all be dead, or seriously injured, right?

'Crashed into the charts (See also:'Crash-landed in the charts)'

One has to wonder whether the artists concerned were travelling somewhere else when they made their unscheduled and evidently near-disastrous appearance in the charts. Flying over the Alps when both engines failed and they were forced to attempt a dangerous landing in the top five? Or on their way to their country pile in a helicopter when an engine malfunction meant they had no option but to head for the nearest landing pad, which happened to be number 12 in the hit parade? Have they made a full recovery from this terrifying and violent encounter with Reggie Yates?

FESTIVALS

'Weather of biblical proportions'
But don't bother looking in the Bible for it. There's precious little mention of intermittent showers, mud, tents and indie-rock.

'Festival survival guide'
Because – ha ha! – conditions are – ha ha! – so bad you might DIE! Ha ha! Except they're not and you won't.

'One guy got trenchfoot one year'
His foot went a little bit manky after walking around barefoot in mud for three days like a clueless berk. Then he went home.

'One year a bloke fell into the long drop toilets'
But no-one's ever met him.

'In one of the muddy years someone accidentally filled the Glastonbury dance tent full of shit by pressing 'blow' instead of 'suck''
But no-one actually saw it happen, the machines don't work like that, and… oh, believe what you like, it's only rock'n'roll, not bloody *Newsnight*.

'Like The Somme'
Where hundreds of thousands of people died in a First World War battle, in stark contrast to a festival, where hundreds of thousands of people were mildly inconvenienced by inclement weather while watching bands in a field.

'Brave the toilets'
Something that the people who wrote this didn't have to do, as they were backstage with luxurious flushing portaloos.

SOME MIGhT SAy

GETTING IT WRONG ABOUT MUSIC SINCE 380 BC

'Any musical innovation is full of danger to the whole state, and ought to be prohibited. When modes of music change, the fundamental laws of the state always change with them.'

Plato, *The Republic*, 380 BC

'Beethoven's Second Symphony is a crass monster, a hideously writhing wounded dragon, that refuses to expire, and though bleeding in the Finale, furiously beats about with its tail erect.'

**Review in Vienna newspaper
Zeitung fur die Elegente Welt, 1804**

'The Finale… is to me for the most part dull and ugly… oh, the pages of stupid and hopelessly vulgar music!'

**Beethoven's Ninth Symphony, reviewed by Philip Hale,
Musical Record, Boston, 1 June, 1899**

'My dear Mozart, it is too exquisite for our ears; there are far too many notes in it.'

**Emperor Joseph II of Austria on *The Seraglio*
after a performance in Vienna, *1782***

'Is Wagner actually a man? Is he not rather a disease? Everything he touches he makes ill: he has made music sick.'

Friedrich Nietzsche on Richard Wagner, 1889

'Liszt's orchestral music is an insult to art. It is gaudy musical harlotry, savage and incoherent bellowings.'

Franz Liszt, reviewed in *The Boston Gazette,1872*

'The concert began with Schubert's unfinished symphony, which on this occasion ought to have been his uncommenced symphony.

G.B. Shaw on Schubert's *Unfinished Symphony*,1893

'Such an astounding lack of talent united to such pretentiousness, never before existed.'

Tchaikovsky on Richard Strauss, 1888

'(Jazz was) invented by demons for the torture of imbeciles…'

**Jazz, as described by Dr Henry van Dyke,
Princeton University, 1921**

*y*ou may have been labouring under the misty-eyed impression that the 1960s was a pretty good period for pop music. But you obviously have this false impression of the Sixties because, as the saying goes, you weren't there. Many of those who were took a decidedly dimmer view of the decade and the (counter) cultural riches it offered up to them. Take off your rose-tinted Lennon specs and consider these thought-provoking contemporary opinions...

the STinKING SiXTiES

12.

THE GOLDEN AGE OF POP...
OR WAS IT?

'Fuzzy and undisciplined, complete chaos.'

**The Rolling Stones, 'I Wanna Be Your Man' (single),
reviewed in *Disc*, 1963**

'Visually, they are a nightmare: tight, dandified Edwardian beatnik suits and great pudding-bowls of hair. Musically they are a near disaster, guitars and drums slamming out a merciless beat that does away with secondary rhythms, harmony and melody. Their lyrics (punctuated by nutty shouts of yeah, yeah, yeah!) are a catastrophe, a preposterous farrago of Valentine-card romantic sentiments.'

**The Beatles' *Ed Sullivan Show* TV appearance,
as reported in *Newsweek*, February 1964**

'BEATLES BOMB ON TV... [they] could not carry a tune across the Atlantic... 75 per cent publicity, 20 per cent haircut, and 5 per cent lilting lament.'

**The Beatles' *Ed Sullivan Show* TV appearance,
as reported in the *International Herald Tribune,* 1964**

Stevie Wonder, 'Kiss Me Baby'
'Stevie Wonder? I honestly fail to see why there's all this fuss about his records. He's a good harmonica player, but I don't reckon him much.'

**The Rolling Stones' Brian Jones reviews the singles,
Melody Maker, 27 March 1965**

'THANK GOD WE WON'T GET THIS SIX-MINUTE BOB DYLAN SINGLE IN BRITAIN.'
'Dylan is saddled with a quite horrific backing dominated by syrupy strings, amplified guitar and organ... the monotonous melody line and Dylan's expressionless intoning just cannot hold the interest for what seems like the six longest minutes since the invention of time.

My copy of the disc bears the legend "Prod. By Tom Wilson." Somebody should have prodded Mr. Wilson until he agreed to lock the backing group in the cellar until the session was over.'

Bob Dawbarn previews Bob Dylan's 'Like A Rolling Stone',
***Melody Maker,* 1965**

'Bobby Dylan?... a youth of mediocre talent. Only a non-critical audience, nourished on the watery pap of pop music could have fallen for such tenth-rate drivel.'

Ewan MacColl, *Sing Out!* magazine, March 1965

Bob Dylan, 'Can You Please Crawl Out Your Window'

'This bloke annoys me – he started out writing great stuff but he still insists on releasing this meaningless material. So much stuff on his albums is good, it's stupid that he should bring all this weird gear on his singles.'

The Kinks' Dave Davies reviews the singles,
***Melody Maker*, 22 January 1966**

'REALLY, IT'S A LOAD OF RUBBISH.'

'Love You Too' [sic], 'George wrote this – he must have quite a big influence on the group now. This sort of song I was doing two years ago...'

'Yellow Submarine', This is a load of rubbish, really. I take the mickey out of myself on the piano and play stuff like this. I think they know it's not that good.'

'She Said She Said', This song is in to restore confidence in old Beatles sound. That's all.'

'And Your Bird Can Sing', 'Don't like this. The song's too predictable. It's not a Beatles song at all.'

'I Want To Tell You', 'This helps the LP through though it's not up to The Beatles standard.'

'Tomorrow Never Knows', 'Listen to all those crazy sounds! It'll be popular in discotheques. I can imagine they had George Martin tied to a totem pole when they did this.'

[In summary] 'This is the first Beatles LP I've really listened to in its entirety but I must say there are better songs on *Rubber Soul.*'

The Kinks' Ray Davies reviews The Beatles' *Revolver* **LP track by track in** *Disc & Music Echo*, **August 1966**

To which the obvious response is: if he hasn't listened to any other Beatles albums, then how would he know?

The Beach Boys, *'Good Vibrations'*

'Too complex… it's probably a good record but who's to know? You have to play it about 90 bloody times to hear what they're singing about!'

The Who's Pete Townshend reviews the singles,
***Disc & Music Echo*, October 1966**

'What is all this nonsense about Brian Wilson? Why is he hailed as a musical genius? Compared to Ray Davies he is a nincompoop. Wilson's lyrics are nothing short of ridiculous. "I'm dreaming of good vibrations," means nothing at all.'

Letter to *NME*, **November 1966**

The Byrds, 'So You Want To Be A Rock'n'roll Star'

'I don't know. I think by now they should be getting off that style of 12-string guitar and that particular brand of harmony. They really should be splitting from that scene because they'll end up finding themselves caught up in it.'

Paul McCartney reviews the singles, *Melody Maker*, **January 1967**

Nancy and Frank Sinatra, 'Somethin' Stupid'

'No – my God, Sinatra has really gone downhill. He's gone so far he'll never come back – for me. Maybe he's fooling around in his old age and I wish he would stop. He had some beautiful records out before *Strangers In The Night* and, my God, he went mad after that.'

Scott Walker reviews the singles, *Melody Maker*, **18 March 1967**

Otis Redding, 'Day Tripper'

'Day Tripper? [NB – the reviewer is not initially told whose record he/she is reviewing.] It's probably somebody really crappy like Otis Redding. It is – oh great, I've got another one!… that's terrible, take it off. I dislike Otis Redding because he's so inaudible and his records are so bad.'

Scott Walker again, *Melody Maker*, 18 March 1967

'What the hell are The Beatles trying to do to pop music. On listening to their new album I was so shocked that I lost all my appreciation of The Beatles' talents. Any normal musical minded person could never hope to like this kind of stuff.

If this is a new era the group are trying to create, then they have my praise, but to try and sell the public rubbish like this [Sergeant Pepper], then they are spitting into the faces of their fans.'

Letter from Bob Jackson, fan review, *Melody Maker*, 27 May 1967

'Like an over-attended child, *Sergeant Pepper* is spoiled. It reeks of horns and harps, harmonica quartets, assorted animal noises, and a 41-piece orchestra… an album of special effects, dazzling but ultimately fraudulent'.

The Beatles, *Sergeant Pepper*, reviewed by Richard Goldstein, *New York Times*, 18 June 1967

'What a pathetic state the pop scene has got to when you have to look like Frank Zappa to sell records. Flower power is only another craze started up by the Yanks and as usual our gullible fans and groups have fallen for it. Thank God for Tom Jones.'

Letter from E.H. Tull, *Melody Maker*, 9 September 1967

'Sounds like a bird singing. I think he gets the crowds at it – he's a crowd worker, but he doesn't appeal to me. I think James Brown mania has been and gone. He's a live performer more than a recording artist.'

Cream's Ginger Baker reviews the singles, Melody Maker, 8 July 1967

'I am fed up with all psychedelic trash passed off as music on the young generation. The strange noises of hippy music cannot compare with the professionalism and good taste of the Bachelors, Cliff Richard, and Englebert Humperdinck, the greatest pop stars of today.'

Letter from Suzanne Worsley, *Melody Maker*, September 1967

'The Beatles do not attempt to reproduce their electronic music in dance halls and on the concert stage. Procul Harum does and so does Pink Floyd. It will not work. In person Pink Floyd, for all its electronic interest, is simply dull in a dance hall following Big Brother and Janis Joplin.'

Ralph J. Gleason, *Rolling Stone*, 20 January 1968

'Its weakest point is the material. Some of the songs meander and lack real melodic substance.'

Love, *Forever Changes*, reviewed by Jim Bickhart, *Rolling Stone*, 10 February 1968

'Whether the man is a poet or not, he is not necessarily a songwriter... I don't think I could ever tolerate all of [this album]. There are three brilliant songs, one good one, three qualified bummers, and three are the flaming shits.'

Leonard Cohen, *Songs Of Leonard Cohen*, reviewed by Arthur Schmidt, *Rolling Stone*, 9 March 1968

Then again, the billboard ads for the album, which pronounced 'James Joyce is alive and living in Montreal, and his name is Leonard Cohen' had kind of asked for it.

The Bee Gees, 'Words'

'Certainly not as good as 'Massachusetts'... now they seem to be trying to repeat the dose. They are just not progressing.'

George Best (yes, that George Best), *Melody Maker*, April 1968

Reports that the Bee Gees responded by saying, 'Yes George, and you just lost the league title to Manchester City, you pissed-up prima donna' sadly cannot be confirmed.

The Doors, 'The Unknown Soldier'

'It's not the sort of thing teenagers want to hear. They don't want to hear military drum beats. God no... I'm sorry... that record doesn't mean anything.'

Johnny Cash reviews the singles, *Melody Maker*, 11 May 1968

'Like Flower Power, the Hoola Hoop [sic] and silent movies, the psychedelic thing has run its course'.

Tony Macaulay on Pink Floyd, *New Musical Express*, 27 April 1968

'All that can be said about The Beatles has been said.'

**Keith Emerson of The Nice reviews 'Hey Jude',
Melody Maker, 31 August 1968**

'Side two is a disaster... the slump begins with "Because", which is a rather nothing song... "Sun King" is probably the worst thing The Beatles have done since they changed drummers... so heavily overproduced that they are hard to listen to... why bother to release it at all?

Surely they must have enough talent and intelligence to do better than this? Or do they?'

**The Beatles, *Abbey Road*, reviewed by Ed Ward,
Rolling Stone, 15 November 1969**

'People who buy it will play it nigh and day for a week, then most will file it away under 's', and forget about it if they saw through it though,they'd skip the first three steps and just forget about it altogether.'

Santana, *Santana*, reviewed in *Rolling Stone*, October 1969

SOME MIGHT SAY

LOVE, SEX, INTELLIGENCE (OR MAYBE JUST THE FIRST TWO)

'I just wanna f**k my mother basically. Always have done. Not so much now because she's getting a bit older, she's losing her grip on her looks. She's a cute little French girl.'

Jean-Jacques Burnel, The Stranglers, 1979

'Because there's AIDS I must not fuck? Okay… but I will fuck because I do not believe I use sex wrongfully. When you are reincarnated and you have been using sex for evil purposes you'll be reincarnated as a homosexual.'

Fela Anikulapo Kuti, 1985

He also condemned condoms as 'un-African'. He would later die of AIDS in 1997. No news on his reincarnation as yet.

'I hate to see chicks perform. Hate it… Because they whore themselves. Especially the ones that don't wear anything. They f**king whore themselves.'

Bob Dylan, *Rolling Stone*, 1987

'We treat groupies like shit because that's what they are.'

Slash, Guns N' Roses, 1989

'I'm a bisexual man who's never had a homosexual experience'.

Suede's Brett Anderson, 1992

Much the same as I see myself as a semi-professional women's beach volleyball player who has never played the game professionally and is not a woman.

'I'm a bisexual man who has never had a heterosexual experience.'

Suede's openly gay drummer Simon Gilbert, 1993

'An abortion can cost a ballin' nigga up to 50gs maybe a 100. Gold diggin' bitches be getting pregnant on purpose. #STRAPUP my niggas!'

Kanye West, via Twitter, 2011

'I have this weird thing that if I sleep with someone they're going to take my creativity from me through my vagina.'

Lady Gaga, *Vanity Fair*, September 2010

it is always a tempting challenge to present a comprehensive history spanning 50-odd years of rock'n'roll. But that would take time, money and complicated explanation which would be a right old turn-off for everyone. So, to simplify things a bit, we will take the traditional approach favoured by all media outlets and boil it down to a nice potted history of music that everyone agrees with, and irons out any difficult bits.

But don't worry if even this is a bit much to digest in one sitting. We've put the important bits you need to remember as aide-mémoires in **bold,** because they were **seminal, iconic moments** of the era.

By joining together these symbolic moments, images and buzz phrases, you can build your own completely fatuous, facile and largely pointless join-the-dots story of 50-odd years of rock'n'roll. So, anyway, here's the official, as-seen-on-TV version of pop history in full. Don't blink, or you might end up in the next decade...

the BOLLOCKS guIDE tO POP hiSTORy

13.

THE COMPLETE HISTORY OF ROCK'N'ROLL – ABRIDGED!

1950s

Nothing happened before 1956. Britain had only just been released from **rationing**, everyone was old and no one did anything except fight in wars. **Teenagers** were amazed suddenly to be able to eat sweets and **listen to the wireless under the bedcovers**[1]. You might want to wheel out John Lennon's quote about how **'Before Elvis there was nothing.'**[2] Well, actually, tell a lie, there was **skiffle**, a genre which boasts only one recorded exponent on planet Earth, in the shape of **Lonnie Donegan. Probably singing 'Rock Island Line'.** Then it was forgotten overnight because **Elvis Presley** was so amazing that he **wasn't allowed to be filmed below the hip.** (You might want to show some film of him below the hip, playing in front of an audience of screaming girls, to show us why.) A generation of British kids were inspired by him, and went to **The Two 'I's coffee bar in Soho** but all they could see there was Tommy Steele, Joe Brown and **Cliff Richard**, although he was actually quite cool back then, you know. **Cliff thought Elvis was great and wanted to be like him,** but he was also actually quite cool himself, you know, in contrast to the appalling old tosspot you know of now. However, the fact he was the best the British could come up with is kind of an unspoken illustration of how crap and unoriginal British music was. Then **Elvis went into the Army**, his haircut providing a neatly symbolic image of rebellion finally knuckling down and conforming, and everyone **went back to sleep… until 1963.**

Unless you want to count the emergence of **Motown**, which might be an idea, since it was the only interesting thing that anyone remembers happening in pop for the next five years, and you can probably get hold of some nice footage of **The Supremes on a TV pop show**[3].

---

1. Or did that come later? Well, at some point anyway, no point in nit-picking.
2. Which he didn't actually say. He said if there'd been no Elvis there'd be no Beatles and everyone took it to mean something else. But let's press on…
3. They actually first emerged in the mid-1960s but they had Diana Ross in, so they take precedence over all those other anonymous muppets.

1960s

Elvis came out of the army right on cue at the start of the 1960s, and was all boring and ballady for a while, performing in **rubbish films.** Nothing was happening in pop except for boring old showbiz crooners (like Pat Boone) and the British rock'n'rollers had become **showbiz bores** too (*see* **Tommy Steele grinning like a berk**).

So, thank god something was happening in **Liverpool**. It's time to picture **The Beatles in The Cavern** and some **screaming girls chasing after them** a couple of years later.

They broke America by **waving from the top of some plane steps** and **doing some press conferences**. America liked them because **they needed cheering up after JFK got shot**. That's right, all of them did. The whole of America. The Beatles were **the boys next door who you could bring home to mum,** but **The Rolling Stones** were **the rebels**. Their gigs ended in riots and they offered a raw, British update on **the blues**[4].

They formed part of **The British invasion**, wherein a montage of British groups such as The Kinks, The Who and The Animals all played to screaming girls in black and white. But everything was about to change because the **Vietnam War** produced footage of **forests being bombed and American soldiers pouring out of planes**, the reaction to which was the **hippy** movement which involved lots of **girls dancing weirdly in fields** while flashing **peace signs** and wearing **colourful clothes** as Scott MacKenzie's 'San Francisco' played in the background.

The Beatles released *Sergeant Pepper* and revolutionised music *again*, and **Jimi Hendrix played the guitar with his teeth, then set fire to it.** Maybe Lulu can remember something about that, she's usually up for any TV she gets offered. However, the **hippy dream** soon **turned sour,** as reflected by **Brian Jones dying and Mick Jagger in a twatty frock releasing lots of butterflies in Hyde Park.**

---

4. Ah yes, the Blues. Not sure how to deal with that one. Just mentioning them in the context of the Stones should be fine. Anyway, it all happened before the 1950s, so strictly speaking it's disqualified.

1970s

The Sixties died at Altamont when someone got **killed** at a **Rolling Stones gig** in America because Mick Jagger was singing '**Sympathy For The Devil**'. It then died even more when The Beatles **split up** on a **rooftop**. And several rock stars then died in America[5], which was the **hangover** after the **party** that was the Sixties.

Nothing then happened in music, and everything was complete rubbish for years. Then, as a reaction to Britain **joining the EU**[6] or something, **glam rock** was invented (by **Gary Glitter doing his Frankie Howerd-stung-by-a-wasp impression,** and **Mud doing 'Tiger Feet'**). It was awful and embarrassing, played by **bricklayers in Bacofoil,** as proved by the **bloke from The Sweet pouting at the camera** on *Top Of The Pops*[7].

However, even that was preferable to **prog rock** which was **Rick Wakeman dressed as a wizard**, on ice. This clip of **Keith Emerson sticking a knife in his piano** might look quite exciting but it was actually all **really boring,** as we can see from this footage of **three trucks going down the motorway in convoy with** 'Emerson', 'Lake' and 'Palmer' on them.

No one in the world who was ever cool liked any music at all during the years 1970–76 except for **Davidbowieandroxymusic**[8] who were brilliant and weird and exciting (check out their **performance of 'Virginia Plain'** on *Top Of The Pops*). Although it may bear a superficial resemblance to other glam rock footage, it is in fact totally different because, as we've mentioned, Davidbowieandroxymusic were cool. Oh and **Lou Reed** and **Iggy** and the **New York Dolls** were alright and, like, really influential on what was to come.

Confusingly, **Northern soul** also happened[9], which was **blokes in tight t-shirts doing high kicks** in a hall in Wigan. No one knows exactly when it happened but **Wayne Hemingway and Stuart Maconie** thought it was great even though they were probably about nine at the time. Still, it's kind of a bit neither-here-nor-there within our narrative so we'll move swiftly on.

Meanwhile, **the Winter of Discontent** lasted the whole of the 1970s. As you can see from well-worn BBC footage of **binbags piled up in the street**[10], everyone's binbags were piled up in the street, **strikes** and

power cuts happened constantly and **the three day week**[11] stretched over 10 whole years, blighting the country.

As a reaction to that, even though most of it hadn't happened yet, **punk rock** was invented. Overnight, everyone **burned their prog rock records** (which no one cool had ever listened to anyway) and became punks with mad hair and leather jackets and safety pins through their noses on the King's Road, sticking two fingers up at the camera.

At this exact moment, the **Sex Pistols** swore at TV presenter **Bill Grundy** and then **signed a record contract outside Buckingham Palace while sticking two fingers up at the camera** and it was all brilliant. All of it. All of punk rock. There was no bad punk rock. And no good prog rock.

However, at the same time, some people in the North had seen **Kraftwerk**. As a reaction to it being **grim up North** (as it also was in the rest of the country but Northerners have the right to go on about it) they decided to make music that reflected the **harsh dullness of life in industrial cities** by inventing **synth pop** which was kind of harsh, dull and robotic but also, you know, quite poppy.

It was also a reaction to the brave new world of Mrs Thatcher winning the general election, which hadn't happened yet. It was good of her to get in at the end of the Seventies because we can refer to her 'influence' almost entirely in connection to the 1980s.

---

5. You know, Jimi Hendrix, Jim Morrison, Janis Joplin, Brian Jones, all that mob. Maybe include a few newspaper headlines if you're desperate.

6. Actually the EEC, but same difference. Later the Labour government would **go cap in hand** to them for more money. Or was that the World Bank or someone? Probably doesn't matter.

7. Actually **Marc Bolan** and the odd bit of **Slade** are OK to like, but you can't include the latter because it's not Christmas.

8. They were in fact two separate acts, David Bowie and Roxy Music, but it's rare in this context for anyone to refer to them separately. If you must do that, maybe check out on YouTube **Bowie licking Mick Ronson's guitar.** Boy George can probably be roped in to say it was a **seminal moment.**

9. Well you know, it was kind of an ongoing thing from the late Sixties to the early Eighties, it says here, on Wikipedia, but that kind of makes out that there was other stuff going on that involved people apparently oblivious to the main events, so maybe it's best to ignore it completely.

10. Well, they were in London anyway, for a couple of weeks, which in media coverage terms is the equivalent of a decade's worth of bubonic plague breaking out anywhere else.

11. Oh God it's complicated. Something to do with having to save on electricity because of electricity strikes so everyone had to take two days off work every week. Actually happened in 1974 whereas the other stuff was about five years later but must we really split hairs?

The **Winter of Discontent** ended on 1 January 1980 with **Thatcher waving outside 10 Downing Street** after being elected. However, everything was still rubbish, as proved by the video for **'Ghost Town' by The Specials** which sums up both the ska revival and the inner-city **riots**, which featured **petrol bombs exploding against riot shields** and a **policeman walking away with a wounded head** while listening to 'Ghost Town' by The Specials. Again. Some people didn't give a toss, though, including **a load of people in make-up outside a club**. They were the **new romantics**, and **Robert Elms** thought they were great even though they **turned people away from nightclubs** for not wearing make-up. **Spandau Ballet** were in them, and they wore **kilts**.

All this pop was much more glamorous, and was a wonderful example of escapism from the grim realities of Thatcher's Britain (as displayed in the video for **'Ghost Town' by The Specials**) and also a vulgar endorsement of those Thatcherite values, as exemplified by **Duran Duran fannying about on a yacht** in the video for 'Rio', followed by Wham! pouring cocktails into a swimming pool in the **'Club Tropicana' video**.

The decade was not without controversy, however, starting with **Culture Club singing 'Do You Really Want To Hurt Me?'** A talking head BBC3 presenter didn't know whether **Boy George** was a boy or girl but that was a welcome distraction because we were going to **war in the Falklands and no one knew where it was**. Thankfully, **Mrs Thatcher was filmed in a tank with a British flag** on as a neat symbol of everything that was going on[12]. As a result we were all scared of nuclear war, as **Frankie Goes To Hollywood** demonstrated, after having a **dwarf doing a wee off a balcony** in their first music video. **Ronald Reagan and one of the short-lived Russian leaders whose name no one remembers wrestled** in their next one and that says it all. Meanwhile, MTV launched, and played **Michael Jackson's 'Thriller'** video, **Prince's 'When Doves Cry'** video and **Madonna's 'Like A Virgin'** video to demonstrate to us how popular they were.

In stark contrast to that were **pictures of starving children in Africa,** which led to **British rock stars gathered around a mike in a studio** singing **'Feed The World'**...

... And then **USA for Africa** and then **Live Aid** led by **Bob Geldof looking tired and being held shoulder high on stage at Wembley.**

Not everyone joined the party however, such as The Smiths, led by **Morrissey** singing the video to 'What Difference Does It Make?' with **flowers hanging out of his back pocket**[13] .

They were in the minority, though, as **yuppies** ruled Britain, **shouting and waving bits of paper on the stock market floor,** holding **mobile phones the size of housebricks**[14] as **children did the Rubik's Cube in 34 seconds**. These people had **'loadsamoney',** as a comedy character of the same name waving cash around, points out by shouting 'loadsamoney'. They also watched Australian soaps, from which came **Kylie Minogue in a bubble bath singing 'I Should Be So Lucky'.**

Meanwhile, **Acid House** was kicking off in Manchester, with **young men in smiley t-shirts flailing and sweating in a dark nitespot, looking like they're almost definitely on drugs.**

We'd like to mention **Madchester** at this point but we're running out of space to cover everything. That picture of **Shaun Ryder sitting on a giant letter 'E'** should sum everything up nicely, accompanied by 'Step On', even though that was released in 1990.

12. This actually happened in 1986, but it's too perfect a photo not to run.
13. Because you could mention a bit more about indie, but it really meant dick-all to anyone who wasn't a student at the time, and the only reason even The Smiths are being mentioned is because history is written by the winners and no one remembers Paul Young.
14. These were owned by just 22 people, all of them in London, until well into the 1990s but must, by law, be featured in all retrospectives about the Eighties, as if you couldn't move for the bloody things.

'Madchester' was a big deal at the start of the 1990s, but we kind of dealt with that in the last decade and haven't got much time left, so let's move onto **grunge,** which was invented with **Nirvana's 'Smells Like Teen Spirit' video**. This was a **hybrid of punk and heavy metal**[15]. However, Britain soon got sick of all that American stuff and reacted to it (three years later) with **Blur prancing around singing 'Parklife'** and **Oasis singing 'Live Forever' sitting on a wall**. Thus **Britpop** started, paving the way for such great things as **the three blokes from Supergrass in bed singing 'We're Alright'** and **John Humphries reading a story from BBC's** *Six O'Clock News* **with a backdrop of the Blur and Oasis logos**.

That was the Britpop wars, but Take That were also huge around that time, as we can all tell from their 'Could It Be Magic' video where **Robbie Williams pouts and writhes around like a twerp**, Robbie Williams would go on to be very successful as a solo artist[16]. The Spice Girls then shook things up at some point by **arsing around in a pretend posh hotel singing 'Wannabe'** and later gave us **Geri Halliwell in a Union Jack dress**.

Noel Gallagher celebrated winning the Britpop wars by **shaking hands with Tony Blair while holding a glass of champagne at 10 Downing Street**, before playing his **Union Jack guitar**, not to be confused with **Geri Halliwell's Union Jack dress**.

In the midst of all that (but we're not sure quite where) was **trip-hop**, so it might be worth throwing in the **'Unfinished Sympathy' video** at some stage[17]. And **Radiohead released** *OK Computer* in 1997, although

---

15. This genre has not been mentioned since the early 1970s because everyone whose opinions we listened to thought it was rubbish. Guns N' Roses were around and were quite influential in the late 1980s, and arguably paved the way for grunge, but everyone still thought they were rubbish because they were heavy metal, until later on, when it was realised that they were actually really good, as were AC/DC, Black Sabbath, and many others. To acknowledge their belated status as OK to like, many people began to wear their t-shirts as fashion statements.

16. Not that anyone knew this at the time, despite what they subsequently tell you. Everyone actually thought Gary Barlow would turn into 'the new George Michael'. Thank you, fate, for that small mercy.

17. OK, so it's from 1991. No one likes a smart arse.

frustratingly that doesn't really fit in with much else. **Tupac and Biggie** got shot but we're kind of losing interest now because it's all a bit too recent. In fact, shall we bother with anything after 2000?

2000s

Look, we're running out of time and you're probably getting a bit bored. Here's a quick mention of **The Strokes** (they 'revitalised guitar music' despite looking like bored students at a fashion show) then let's briefly cover TV talent shows in which **Will Young was open-mouthed at winning the first** *Pop Idol*, Eminem[18], has a few seconds shoehorned in here, along with **The White Stripes' 'Seven Nation Army' video** because they've split up now and that makes them more important. Let's finish off with **Arctic Monkeys looking like they're playing a gig in school assembly** and then maybe chuck in **Amy Winehouse doing 'Rehab'**, since she's carked it, and **Lady Gaga** cavorting in a hat made from dead marmosets, just so no one can accuse us of being sexist.

Job's a good 'un.

Now make sure you've remembered all that, because I'm not writing it all out again.

18. You could also mention **50 Cent** who was **shot nine times you know** but he quickly went shit so maybe let's skip that.

it's tough going, this business of show. So much so, that sometimes even the most successful performers decide to throw in their incense-perfumed towel, and walk away from it all. Or at least, turn their back on the arduous, bathing-in-the-adoration-of-millions-on-a-nightly-basis touring side of it.

Oddly enough, though, their 'retirements' never seem to last. In this chapter we chart the progress of several prominent names who bowed out at their peak... then bowed back in.

Never SaY nEVER aGaiN

14.

REPORTS OF MY RETIREMENT HAVE BEEN EXAGGERATED (BY ME)

*RETIREMENT

LITTLE RICHARD

1957 Quits to 'serve God' after a scary plane flight. Makes only gospel music for several years.

1962 Performs a British tour with an up-and-coming group called The Beatles as support and bows to demands to play his early, funny stuff.

FRANK SINATRA

1971 Pulls down the curtain on a long career, saying he is going to 'teach.'

1973 Releases new album *Ol' Blue Eyes Is Back*, presumably having found the PGCE course a touch too demanding.

DAVID BOWIE

1973 Announces, at the end of the Ziggy Stardust tour, 'Not only is it the last show of the tour, but it's the last show that we'll ever do.'

1974 The world realises he was just retiring 'in character' as Ziggy when his new single 'Rebel Rebel' is released.

1975 (April) Retires again: 'There will be no more rock and roll records or tours from me. The last thing I want to be is some useless f**king rock singer.'

1975 (November) Releases new single 'Golden Years'.

1987 (roughly) Officially becomes a 'useless f**king rock singer'.

TIMELINE*

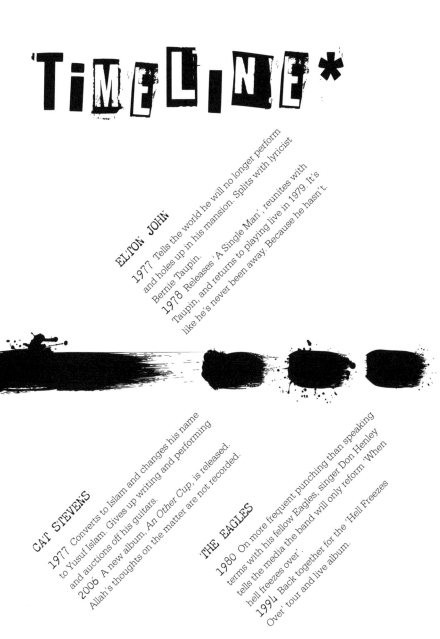

ELTON JOHN

1977 Tells the world he will no longer perform and holes up in his mansion. Splits with lyricist Bernie Taupin.

1978 Releases 'A Single Man', reunites with Taupin, and returns to playing live in 1979. It's like he's never been away. Because he hasn't.

CAT STEVENS

1977 Converts to Islam and changes his name to Yusuf Islam. Gives up writing and performing and auctions off his guitars.

2006 A new album, *An Other Cup*, is released. Allah's thoughts on the matter are not recorded.

THE EAGLES

1980 On more frequent punching than speaking terms with his fellow Eagles, singer Don Henley tells the media the band will only reform 'When hell freezes over'.

1994 Back together for the 'Hell Freezes Over' tour and live album.

THE WHO

1982 They embark on a 'farewell' tour, saying they will no longer play live, due to Pete Townshend's health concerns.

1985 Play at the US Live Aid and, er, forget to stop playing after that.

OZZY OSBOURNE

1992 Announces he is putting his fake fangs in a glass of Steradent after the 'No More Tours' tour.

1996 Embarks on the 'Retirement Sucks' tour.

STATUS QUO

1984 After 20 years together, they announce the 'End of the Road' tour, which will be their last ever shows.

1985 The tears have barely dried on all those denim jackets when they return to the stage to open US Live Aid.

KISS

2000 Gene, Paul and the other two announced a farewell tour only four years after going back into their trademark make-up and reuniting the original line-up.

2002 It turns out an important detail had been unaccountably omitted from their original statement. There had indeed been a farewell, but it had been from original members Ace Frehley and Peter Criss. Gene and Paul duly un-retired, alongside another other two. On well, no hard feelings, eh?

BARBRA STREISAND

2000 Never exactly a committed roadhog at the best of times, Streisand finally calls time on a gruelling schedule of, ooh, roughly two gigs per decade when she vows that a final quartet of televised shows in New York and LA will be her last ever.

2006 Gets an unexpected second wind and announces a string of dates backed by opera catalogue models Il Divo. Confirmed bachelors throughout the world are outraged that they paid half Babs' wardrobe budget for those previous once-in-a-lifetime final shows.

GARTH BROOKS

2002 Quits to 'be at home with my kids'.

2007 Returns to touring and releases a new album two years later. Kids' whereabouts unknown.

LISA SCOTT-LEE

2005 Promises to retire if her new single, 'Electric' doesn't make the top 10. It reaches number 13.

2007 New album *Never Or Now* is released. It doesn't chart. Claims she was 'pushed into' making the retirement promise for a reality TV show. Can we push you again, Lisa?

JAY Z

2003 Announces that his Madison Square Garden show will be a 'retirement party'.

2004 Collaborates with Linkin Park, and performs with them at the Grammies, then admits he is 'un-retiring', calling his hiatus 'The worst retirement ever'. Actually, Jay, you're not even close.

50 CENT

2007 Says he will retire if his album *Curtis* does not sell as many as Kanye West's *Graduation*. It doesn't.

2008 New album, *Before I Self Destruct*, released. No one believes he is about to self destruct.

LILY ALLEN

2010 March. The woman who gave us 'Smile' and 'Fuck You' (not at the same time) bowed out of the musical arena to pursue fashion projects and possibly 'write a musical'.

2010 July. Appears with Jay-Z at London's Wireless festival. Still no official comeback, but put it this way – if you're reading this in 2015 and she still hasn't made another record, I will personally come round to your house and eat your copy of this book.

SOME MIGHT SAY

PHILOSOPHY, POLITICS AND ECONOMICS

'I would go back to play segregated audiences.
We are entertainers and we must entertain these people.
Let South Africa run its own policies.'

Cliff Richard, 1965

'After China takes over the whole world, then the whole
world will know why America's trying so hard in Vietnam.'

Jimi Hendrix, 1967

'Rock stars are fascists. Adolf Hitler was one of the first
rock stars. Think about it. Look at some of his films and see
how he moved. I think he was quite as good as Jagger. It's
astounding. And boy, when he hit that stage, he worked
an audience. Good God!'

David Bowie, 1976

'Old Adolf Hitler wasn't the villain. He never killed a Jew
with his own hands. He never made lampshades out
of human skin. I feel no empathy with the man but look
upon him as the first rock star in a way.'

Lemmy, 1984

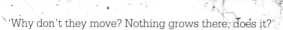

'Why don't they move? Nothing grows there, does it?'

John Lydon on the Ethiopian famine, 1985

'Now with AIDS, it's spread man to man, and all I know is, the parts don't fit!... all I know is, once they start violating, sticking things in places they don't belong, they don't know what they're f***in' with!'

Public Enemy's Chuck D, 1990

'If a woman takes offence to us saying "bitch" that means she must be one.'

Dr Dre, 1994

"America... it is pure devilry them things that go on there. Them 'ave punks, mon, so the oppressors bring another man to blind the youth to the truth. And they call him "John Tra-vol-ta!" '

Bob Marley, 1979

'I think a lot of people are laying down and acting. I don't think there's too much killing any more. I think they're doing a lot of acting and sweating a lot of ketchup on each other... people laying down and throwing ketchup, that's what they're doing.'

James Brown on the problems in South Africa, 1988

I'd like to think that after reading this book, and realising that all your musical heroes are but sawdust Caesars whose reputations crumble into dust at the slightest scrutiny, you will conclude: 'I could do this!' And indeed you can.

Now, admittedly, the hard part, which is writing a melody that will lodge permanently in the cerebral cortex of millions, I can't help you with. But the words? No problem at all. I've put all the key phrases you need in bold.

It goes 'a little something' like this...

sing something simple

15.

OUR FOOLPROOF GUIDE
TO WRITING YOUR OWN SONG

SUBJECT

While you could, in theory, attempt to write a pop song about the misuse of primitive machine gun technology in the Franco-Prussian War, you need to come up with a subject that strikes a chord with the broadest possible audience.

So maybe just refer vaguely to **this love**.

This allows you to refer to it as a person, a union of individuals, or a relationship stretching over a non-specific period of time. You can do anything with **this love** – use it, lose it, take it and make it evergreen, fight for it, fold it up and use it as a paper aeroplane. But whatever you do, you **don't wanna lose it/you/this feeling**.

SETTING

It's always nice to give a sense of place and situation for your song. So why not set it **in the club** (note: Somewhere vaguely cool sounding, not the Batley & district Conservative club), more specifically, **on the floor** (not literally – nothing can ever be achieved in pop by sitting or lying down). Alternatively, if you are expressing negative emotions, you could be **standing in the rain**. You tend to find that this situation is a close relative of feeling **so much pain**. Similarly, there's no harm in your being left **out in the cold** for part of the song, because you can probably get away with a rhyme with the harm it's doing to **your soul**.

The performer might even have reached the point where he/she is **down on my knees**. If so, there's an 81 per cent chance that this will involve **begging you, please**.

DETAILS

If you want to colour in your scene a little, remember that **perfume** must always be **cheap**. **Wine** must always be **red**, as must be a woman's **dress**. **Hair** must always be **blonde**. Unless you're Nick Cave, but that is not possible because… above all, you must **be yourself**. After all, it goes without saying (but say it anyway), **you can't be no one else**.

If you were toying with the idea of 'being' your Auntie Ethel for a month, then spending a few heady days as Archbishop Desmond Tutu before an intense 24 hours inhabiting the turbulent mind and ravaged body of Mark E. Smith, well, sorry, you can't.

IN SUMMARY

Ultimately, though, **my advice** (and you shouldn't need **asking twice**), in any given situation, is simply to **hold on**.

The good thing about this phrase is that it fits all manner of situations from the Israeli-Palestinian conflict to an ingrowing toenail. It is also a neat way of avoiding you directly having to address the problem, rather like pretending to be momentarily called away while in a sticky situation (your marriage is collapsing? Er... **hold on**, I've just got to take this urgent phone call).

And if you **hold on**, then you can **make it**. Again, we're not quite sure what you'll make (par at the Dubai Open? A matchstick model of the Taj Mahal?), but rest assured you can **hold on** to this **good thing we've got**.

And if you feel the need to offer further reassurance, you can simply say: **It's gonna be alright**. Particularly if you make it to the **morning light**.

SIGNING OFF

If you're left in any doubt about how to bring your song neatly to a close, you need to get even simpler, and describe what you are doing, which is, **singin' la la la la la la la**. Or you might be **singin' oooh oooooooooh oooooh** or **I-eeee-I-eeee-I**.

Repeat to fade, and watch the world fall at your feet. You can thank me later.

ACKNOWLE

I'd like to thank a few people for their help in making this book the towering intellectual achievement it is.

Firstly, a debt of gratitude the NUJ's 'Next Big Thing' email collective of fellow under-employed music hacks, whose glittering mind palaces full of musical ephemera I have repeatedly been granted permission to raid.

Respect is also due to the tireless work of archivists such as Rock's Back Pages, Brian McCloskey's Like Punk Never Happened blog and the good old British Library, who have made reams of yellowing archives accessible to future generations who might have cause to wonder just what sort of write-up Pookiesnackenburger got for their debut single in 1981.

I am also indebted to the invaluable research of the web's premier urban myth investigators, Snopes.com, for exposing several of the untruths exposed herein.

I'd also like to express my gratitude to the musicians and music writers featured in the book.

DGEMENTS

While I may mock isolated examples of their creative output in these pages, it doesn't diminish my respect for the passion and expertise that invariably informs what they do. They've only ended up in here because they had the courage to stick their necks out and express their convictions without fear of being ridiculed in a compilation of clangers many decades later. We should all reserve the right to be wrong occasionally.

I should also add a big thank you to drugs and alcohol, both of which have surely had a major part to play in many of the follies I've highlighted here.

And I shouldn't forget to credit my editor, Malcolm Croft, and agent, Susan Smith, for their support and constructive criticism. I ignored it all, as you can see.

And finally, thank you, in a very real sense, for the music. Without a song, and a dance, what are we? Bored, or in my case, unemployed.

And I'd like to apologise again to my mother for swearing, this time in the title. If that isn't proof of rock'n'roll's corrupting influence on a well brought-up and God-fearing young mind, I don't know what is.

Johnny

Created in 2007, Portico publishes a range
of books that are fresh, funny and forthright.

portico

An imprint of Anova Books

CRAP LYRICS

A Celebration of the very worst pop lyrics of all time...EVER!

Johnny Sharp

'Me and my husband were reading it on the beach and we were laughing so much people were moving away thinking we were disturbed.'

Julie Burchill

Crap Lyrics is a hilarious celebration (and occasionally, condemnation) of over 120 of the most ridiculous hooks, lines and stinkers from pop poetry through the modern ages. Johnny Sharp has spent 15 years as a music journalist, and several of those years writing for NME under the name Johnny Cigarettes, so he knows that ridicule is nothing to be scared of. He's serious as cancer when he asks: Are we human, or are we dancer? And where do we go from here? Is it down to the lake, I fear?

Johnny Sharp has trawled half a century of lyrics to find the funniest examples of crippled couplets, outrageous innuendo, mixed metaphors, shameless self-delusion, nefarious nonsense and flagrant filth. Not to mention unforgivable over-use of alliteration.

Paperback: 9781906032593, £7.99 • eBook: 9781907554780